SERVANT
LEADERSHIP

Influencing Others to Get There by Leading a Transformational Life

David Kuhnert

authorHOUSE®

AuthorHouse™
1663 Liberty Drive
Bloomington, IN 47403
www.authorhouse.com
Phone: 1 (800) 839-8640

Published by AuthorHouse 12/06/2016

ISBN: 978-1-5246-5374-3 (sc)
ISBN: 978-1-5246-5373-6 (e)

Library of Congress Control Number: 2016920220

Print information available on the last page.

NIV
Scripture quotations marked NIV are taken from the Holy Bible, New International Version®. NIV®. Copyright © 1973, 1978, 1984 by International Bible Society. Used by permission of Zondervan. All rights reserved. [Biblica]

NKJV
Scripture quotations marked NKJV are taken from the New King James Version. Copyright © 1982 by Thomas Nelson, Inc. Used by permission. All rights reserved.

CONTENTS

Chapter 6 - SEEK AND SHARE TRUTH

Chapter 7 - HANDLING EMOTIONS/SYSTEMS THINKING

Chapter 8 - THE TWO CIRCLES

Chapter 9 - EFFECTIVE COMMUNICATION

Chapter 10 - TYING IT ALL TOGETHER

FOREWORD

This book is a collaboration with Hermann Eben and Trimtab Solutions. It is a derivative of his life work with similar material. This work can be found in the GR8 Leaders material and the GR8 Relationships material that he has published. To find out more, go to GR8leaders.com or GR8relationships.com.

The Author of this book, David Kuhnert, grew up in Northern Wisconsin on a small farm. Shortly after graduating high school in 1988, he joined the army and got married to his wonderful wife Beth. He went to Infantry One Station Unit Training in August of 1988.

His first duty assignment was Fort Ord, CA with the 7th Infantry Division. During his four years at Fort Ord, he deployed to Operation Just Cause in Panama and also deployed to Honduras for five months as part of Joint Task Force Bravo. While stationed in CA from 1988-1992, Dave and Beth welcomed their first two girls, Elizabeth and Katherine into the family.

His next duty assignment was the Sixth Infantry Division at Fort Wainwright, AK. During this three year period from 1993-1995, he earned the rank of Staff Sergeant and welcomed his daughter Amanda and son Joseph to the family.

The Kuhnerts would spend the next four years from 1996-1999 at Fort Bragg, NC in the 82nd Airborne Division. While stationed at Fort Bragg, Dave was deployed to Egypt for seven months. During this tour, get was able to tour parts of Egypt and the Holy Land. After redeploying to Fort Bragg, Dave earned the rank of Sergeant First Class and the Army sent him off to Drill Sergeant School.

Dave graduated from Drill Sergeant School at the top of his class and served as a Drill Sergeant for two years (2000-2001) at Fort Jackson, SC. The plan for the family was to go back to Alaska for the next duty assignment. However, September 11th of 2001 changed the plan. Dave felt the need to go back to Fort Bragg, NC to be in one of the most eligible units to deploy.

After returning to Fort Bragg and the 82nd Airborne Division in 2001, Dave's unit was deployed to Afghanistan. The unit made an impact in several parts of the country from Kandahar to Khowst. The unit returned to the states for six months where Dave was promoted to First Sergeant. The unit was next sent to Fallujah, Iraq for ten months. Upon returning to the states for six months, the unit again received orders to go back to Iraq.

Needing a break, Dave volunteered for ROTC duty at Michigan Tech University in 2006. After moving to Michigan and working with cadets for a year, the Army promoted him to Sergeant Major and sent him to the Air Force Senior NCO Academy where he graduated at the top of his class. The Air Force Academy is a shorter course than the Army's Academy. This shorter course allowed the Army to then send him back to Afghanistan for a year as a Combat Advisor.

The Combat Advisor team he joined came together for training at Fort Riley, KS and then deployed for a year to Kabul, Afghanistan. Dave worked first with the Afghan Army and later the police and high level government officials. After redeploying, Dave was assigned to Fort Riley, KS as a Command Sergeant Major in 2008.

After three years as a Battalion Command Sergeant Major, Dave retired from the Army. He retired in June of 2011 after 23 years of service. He moved to Texas to work in the oilfield in July of 2011. He was hired by CrownQuest Operating where he serves as the Production Manager for an oil and gas operating company. He is also the manager for the CrownQuest Leadership Development Team who coordinates and teaches all of the internal leadership training for the company. They also do leader training for the community and faith based organizations across the country.

Dave's military awards include the Combat Infantryman's Badge (2nd award), the Ranger Tab, Master Parachutist Badge, Air Assault Badge, Expert Infantryman's Badge, Drill Sergeant Badge, the Bronze Star Medal (4th award), the Meritorious Service Medal (4th award) and numerous other awards and decorations. His military and civilian schooling include Ranger School, Drill Sergeant School, the Sergeants Major Academy, Airborne School, Jumpmaster School, Air Assault School, an MBA in Business Management with a human resource focus and numerous other military schools.

CHAPTER 1

The Structure of Leadership and the Framework for Life

Proverbs 3:6 *"Trust in the Lord with all your heart and lean not on your own understanding; in all your ways submit to Him, and He will make your paths straight."*

Servant Leadership Defined

Leadership is thought of in many different ways. When I ask the question of what leadership is, I rarely get the same answer twice. Generally, most of the answers are in the right direction for what a leader is or what a leader should be doing. The Army defines leadership as the art of influencing others to accomplish a mission by providing purpose, motivation and direction in order to improve the organization. John Quincy Adams, the sixth President of the United States, said, "If your actions inspire others to dream more, learn more, do more and become more, you are a leader." For the purposes of this book I am simply going to define leadership as influencing others to get THERE.

Influencing others to get THERE is a very simple definition most of us should be able to remember with relative ease. It utilizes the word influence which I will lay out in great detail later. The definition is others centric and not me centric. It focuses on getting to a predetermined place or goal, a THERE. All of these are characteristics of servant leadership. Although this is not all-encompassing, it is sufficient to describe what servant leadership is all about.

As we look at the definition of leadership, we see that we are influencing others to get to a THERE. The THERE we are trying to get to comes from the basic structure for how life works. We have a THERE, a HERE and a PATH. The THERE is where we are trying to get; this could be a goal or a place in life. The HERE is where you are currently; not just physically but your current reality. Finally, the PATH is what links the HERE to the THERE.

THERE-HERE-PATH

In the picture above, we see Ulysses (U) going toward the top of the mountain. The top of the mountain is his THERE. Ulysses' current reality, HERE, is that he is a good distance from his THERE. The dotted blue line is the PATH he plans to take to get THERE. This is how life works. We have somewhere we want to get to, somewhere we currently are and a plan to move there.

Also in the picture, you see the words Act/Learn/Adjust under the word PATH. This is to help us understand that as we take a step down the PATH, our HERE has just changed and we will need to reassess where we are. Ulysses PATH looks very straight forward but what will happen when he moves over the first rise and comes to an impassable obstacle like a cliff? He will need to alter his PATH from the easy straight line to adjust to the terrain of life. This is what we have to do in life if we want to make progress towards our THERE. We normally think things will be easier than they really are. When we hit an obstacle in life, we need to Act/Learn/Adjust to our new circumstances so that we can use our experience to help us in the future.

There are a couple of different ways to use the THERE-HERE-PATH (THP) process. One way is using THP for the creative process. This helps define where we want to try to be in life. We want to direct our lives through the creative process, deciding where we want to go and what we want to accomplish. Having clarity of our THERE creates structural tension between where we our (HERE) and where we want to be (THERE). This gives us motivation to move from HERE to THERE down the PATH. We would come up with our THERE, figure out our HERE (current reality) and then move from HERE to THERE down the PATH.

The other way to use the THP process is when we are problem solving. Instead of using THP, we would use HERE-THERE-PATH (HTP). This happens when our HERE becomes untenable. We no longer like our current reality (our HERE) and need to change it. To accomplish this, we need to know what about our current reality isn't good, decide we don't want that anymore and choose a new THERE. Once we have our THERE identified, we begin moving down the PATH.

When considering our THERE, it is important for us to have clarity. Clarity creates unity of effort. When we have an absence of clarity, there are normally consequences that follow. When our THERE (goal) is for ourselves, we have to have internal clarity. When the THERE (goal) is for the team, we want to make sure that we have enough external clarity to create a shared vision for all team members. We do this through effective communication. This can also be called vision casting.

When you look at the picture of Ulysses moving towards the mountaintop, think of this from a team perspective. Ulysses represents the team leader and he points to the top of the mountain telling the team that we are going THERE. As he points to the peak, what are the chances that everyone else on the team sees exactly which peak he is referring to? What happens if you think he means the peak on the left and I think he means the peak on the right? Initially we will all be moving down the PATH together but as we get closer to our goal our PATHs will begin to separate. We will begin to have divergent PATHs and all still believe that we are headed to the same place. This will cause a potentially high degree of friction that could destroy the team. Our words matter. We need to communicate with clarity exactly where we are trying to go or what we are trying to achieve to eliminate as much of that friction as possible.

In the military, clarity is talked about for every mission. It has been said that if everyone knows the task and purpose for the operation, they can accomplish any mission. Therefore, every mission statement given in the military contains the task, what is to be accomplished, and the purpose for it. This creates unity of effort and eliminates confusion or friction. Essentially, you begin with the end in mind and backward plan. Once you have stated this purpose, you would create the key milestones needed to reach that end or THERE. This backward planning process is exceptionally good with planning complex operations.

Research shows that we normally have to repeat things 7-11 times in multiple formats for people to finally hear what we are saying. The Bible is a great example of this. God creates something perfect and good, gives it to man with clear expectations and clear consequences and man fails to meet the expectations and has to suffer the consequences. Next, God steps in and redeems his creation and makes it good again. We see this all throughout scripture from the story of Adam and Eve, to Noah and the flood, to Moses and the Exodus, to David, and the list goes on, until the unfolding of the redemptive actions of God in the coming of Christ as a child. God is giving us the framework for the story several times to teach us and get us to listen because He knows that clarity comes through repetition of material in the form of stories and settings.

With our new definition of leadership being *influencing others to get THERE*, let's take a look at leaders. When I ask a group of people who were some of the greatest leaders in the history of the world, I get a good variety of answers. In any group, I typically get George Washington, Abraham Lincoln, Martin Luther King Jr. and the like. The next question is, what made these leaders great? This is usually where the struggle begins. We have to think a little bit harder about what made them great and what greatness is.

What made those leaders great? What set those leaders apart from other leaders? Normally the answer is commitment to the THERE. Leaders have to have commitment to get THERE. What made them great was that they were committed to their THERE, unto death if necessary. They also had a THERE that was great. Having a great cause, or THERE, coupled with the commitment to get THERE is very influential.

The Battle of Little Round Top

The picture above is a depiction of LTC Joshua Chamberlain and the 20th Maine at the Battle of Little Round Top.

In late June of 1863, the Confederate Army under General Robert E. Lee was massing near Gettysburg, PA. Gettysburg would arguably become the key battle of the Civil War. It was the pivotal moment where momentum in the war would change. It was the bloodiest battle of the entire war. It took place on July 1-3 1863 and more Americans would die in this battle than the Revolutionary War, War of 1812 and the Spanish American War combined. More than 55,000 lives were lost in those three days.

The 20th Maine commanded by LTC Joshua Chamberlain, was ordered to get to Gettysburg as quickly as they could. They marched 100 miles in four days to get there. They were carrying heavy loads in the summer heat as they marched towards what they knew would be a large battle.

Prior to the war, Joshua Chamberlain was a school teacher in Maine who was very passionate about freeing the slaves. He was convinced by his friends and students to purchase a commission and join the military. Chamberlain bought his commission and formed the 20th Maine. His younger brother also joined and became Joshua's Aide de Camp.

On July 1st 1863, the battle for Gettysburg began. The cavalry unit under General John Buford managed to seize the high ground near Gettysburg called Cemetery Ridge. They held the high ground through the first night and prevented the southern units from gaining a foothold. This would prove decisive over the next two days.

As the 20th Maine was moving towards Gettysburg on July 1st, they ran into 13 Union Soldiers heading in the wrong direction. They stopped the men and Chamberlain's brother interviewed them to find out why they were moving away from the battle. They explained that they had been separated from their unit. This was obviously not the case so Chamberlain's brother reminded him that the penalty for desertion is to face the firing squad. Chamberlain decided to talk to the men himself. He found out that all 13 of them were sharpshooters and hailed from Maine as well. He told the men that the 20th

7

Maine was heading to Cemetery Ridge and intended to fight. They were going to do their duty that they had sworn an oath to do. Chamberlain told them that they were welcome to join the 20th Maine but if they came along they had to fight. If they chose not to come along, they could head straight back to Maine because he wouldn't shoot good Maine men. After some deliberation, all 13 men decided to join Chamberlain and the 20th Maine as they headed towards Gettysburg.

As the 20th Maine approached Gettysburg, Colonel Vincent, Chamberlain's commanding officer, told him that Cemetery Ridge was now being manned by most of the Union forces but the ridge was shaped like a "J" and at the end of the "J" was a hill called Little Round Top. This hill had unintentionally been left unmanned and if the Confederates were to put cannons on top of it they would be able to fire straight down the Union line, forcing them to retreat. He told Chamberlain to defend Little Round top and "Hold at all Hazards."

Understanding his mission, Chamberlain moved his 386 man battalion to the crest of Little Round Top. He positioned his men in two ranks. Their lines formed an "L" shape. At the center of the "L", where the line angled, Chamberlain positioned himself next to a large boulder. This boulder would serve to anchor his line. He had to use this "L" formation to prevent the Confederates from coming around their flank.

Shortly after moving into position, two Confederate regiments from Alabama commanded by General Hood began to press their attack up the hill. The fighting was fierce. The Confederates advanced to the point where the muzzles of their rifles could have touched those of the 20th Maine. They could not dislodge Chamberlain and his men so they retreated back down the hill.

The 20th Maine had held this key terrain but they were beat up. The vegetation on the thickly wooded hill had been mowed down from the thousands of musket rounds that had been fired. There was a heavy smoke filling the air from all of the musket fire and small fires that had started. Many of

Chamberlain's men were on the ground dead or wounded and all of them were thirsty and tired.

General Hood reinforced his two Alabama regiments with a regiment from Texas and pressed the attack again. This time he decided to try to bring one regiment further around the flank of the 20th Maine to get behind them. Chamberlain saw the Texas regiment moving around the end of his "L" formation so ordered his second rank of men to execute a complex side-step maneuver to extend his line. They did all of this while under fire. As the Confederates on the flank began charging up the hill, the 13 sharpshooters that chose to join the 20th Maine began to decimate the Confederate officers and leaders. By all accounts they poured such lethal fire into the Confederates that they prevented the 20th Maine from breaking on that second charge. Despite the accurate fire, the 20th Maine was pushed out of position five times during this charge but managed to fight back into positon each time.

The aftermath of this second charge was hard for Chamberlain to stomach. One third of his men were dead or dying around him. He had been wounded twice. He had been shot in his sword's scabbard which left a large contusion and a stray round had hit the boulder he stood next to, sending rock fragments into his ankle. His men were tired and down to less than two musket rounds per man.

Reality of the gravity of the situation had set in for Chamberlain. They could not survive the third charge that was forming down the hill. Chamberlain brought his company commanders together and told them to have the men fix bayonets. They would charge down the hill into the enemy. As they charged, the far flank of the "L" would swing like a barn door until they were all on line and charge down the hill together in one line.

The command was given. Chamberlain ordered the charge and leapt over the boulder with saber drawn. The 20th Maine bravely charged down the hill and caught the Confederate regiments by complete surprise. Not understanding what was happening, the Confederates retreated from the battle.

The 20th Maine had held Little Round Top.

The next day, July 3rd, General Lee gave the orders for General Pickett to march his men across the wheat field and assault the ridgeline in one last effort to win the battle. This became known as Pickett's Charge. General Pickett's men were decimated and the Union had secured a major victory in the Civil War that would shift the momentum to the North. The confederates retreated across the river and the battle was over on July 4th 1863.

Joshua Chamberlain received the Medal of Honor for his actions at Little Round Top. He later presided over the surrender of General Lee at Appomattox Court House where he was criticized for having his men salute the defeated Confederates. As it would turn out, this simple act of respect would go a long way during the restoration after the war. Chamberlain would go on to serve four consecutive terms as the Governor of Maine and later died in 1914.

Let's examine this story and see the how THP process is involved. What was the THERE for the 20th Maine? The THERE would have been to hold at all hazards. Colonel Vincent did a great job giving Chamberlain the clarity of the THERE by describing why Little Round Top was so important in the defense of Cemetery Ridge. Chamberlain understood what was expected of him and his regiment along with the gravity of the situation. They knew their task and purpose. They had clarity of the THERE.

What was the HERE for Chamberlain and the 20th Maine? We know that their current reality consisted of them holding key terrain. They also had the 13 sharpshooters attached. They were probably physically exhausted. They were in the "L" shape formation defending the end of the Union line and after the second Confederate charge, they were down to two rounds per man and a good number of the men were dead or wounded.

What was the PATH for Chamberlain and his men? We can see Chamberlain's decision to do what he thought was best to support the THERE. The PATH was to fix bayonets and charge down the hill while swinging the flank of the unit to come on line like a barn door.

Chamberlain's story helps us see the THP very clearly. Examine your life. Do you have a THERE you are trying to accomplish? Do you have a good sense of your HERE or current reality? Have you laid out a PATH to accomplish your THERE?

A Transcendent THERE

We normally have many THEREs in life for goals we are trying to achieve. These may be job related, family, financial or even social. However, we ultimately want to have a THERE that transcends these goals. We call this our Transcendent THERE. By definition, you can never reach something that is transcendent. We want to have a THERE that gives us a direction in life that cannot be reached.

Most businesses have a THERE, a mission statement, a vision statement, or a purpose statement to create a shared vision for where they want their organization to head. When all employees understand this statement, it creates a shared vision for unity of effort. If it is important enough for a money making venture to have a THERE, why wouldn't we want a THERE for our own lives, our marriages and our children?

We have so many little goals in our lives that are all good. However, we need a Transcendent THERE to create an integrated life. Only through focusing on our Transcendent THERE, can we integrate all of our goals together and prevent oscillation between goals. A good example of this is family and work. We tend to focus on one, like work, because it is suffering and then ignore the other (family) to some degree. This causes family to suffer so then we oscillate back in the other direction like a pendulum on a clock. This is the pattern many people follow throughout life. However, when we focus on our transcendent THERE; we can pull all other goals into line. They all become integrated. Doing this will help us focus on what is important.

Having clarity of our Transcendent THERE, and focusing on it, prevents us from oscillating between two goals. It helps us do what is right when life gets difficult. When we communicate our Transcendent THERE with the people in our lives, it helps them better understand what we are trying to do; the direction we are trying to head.

Now we will try to answer the question the intellectuals and scholars from the beginning of time have attempted to answer: What is the meaning of life? I will reframe the question to, what should my Transcendent THERE be?

Mark Twain said, "The two greatest days in a man's life are the day he is born and the day he figures out why."

As of 2016, 76% of Americans profess to be Christian. 24% can tell you why they are on this earth. However, less than 5% have a good transcendent THERE. The other 19% would list wealth, title or position, or some other material gain as their purpose on this earth.

What about happiness? Would that be a viable THERE? What does it mean to be happy? What does it take to make you happy? If when we think of happy we are thinking of joyfulness or contentedness, then happiness is a THERE moving in the right direction. However, we usually use happiness as another word for fulfilled appetites. What we tend to drift towards when we say we want to be happy, is fulfilling our personal appetites. This may be money, title, sex, or any other worldly lust. These usually don't make good THEREs. These types of goals are achievable and then lead to the "now what?" problem. When we achieve a goal that has been our life-long focus, our THERE, we tend to ask, "Now what?" We start to lose our focus of what we are doing in life because we have lost our purpose. We have achieved it. Then we want more. If you wanted to be a millionaire, made it your focus in life and then you save a million dollars, you would probably want more. It will never be enough.

Have you had anything in your life become your major THERE and then accomplished it? Maybe it was a sports competition, running a race, a job title or your children. When you finish the competition, earn the new title or your children leave home, you go through a bit of a setback. Maybe even a depression like empty nest syndrome. All of this is the result of having a THERE you can achieve instead of a transcendent THERE. You were focused on the wrong thing.

During my time in the Army, we would spend a lot of time preparing to deploy, fight and win our nation's battles. With a combat deployment looming, my THERE quickly became getting everyone home safely. This became my sole focus. Even before we would deploy, I would be so focused on making sure everyone was trained and had everything they needed that, to my family, I might as well already be gone. My mind was already deployed. Once we would get in country, my focus became even more intense. I think most people would agree that this is a very noble and good focus to have. I agree that it would be a good goal but shouldn't have become my THERE.

Once we redeployed, I would go through a depression. Whether everyone made it home in one piece or not, the deployment had ended. Now what? My whole purpose and focus in life had become getting everyone home. It was now complete. Now what? It would take months of going through the motions in life to figure out what my next THERE should be. If I would have had a better, more Transcendent THERE, I would have recognized the reintegration into a more "normal" life as just another stepping stone in life and would still have been moving towards my Transcendent THERE.

We can see this in raising children as well. Many times our focus as parents becomes our children. That focus takes over our lives and becomes our THERE. We know we should be focused on God first and then our spouse. Children are temporary members of the team and although they are important, they should not be our sole focus in life. Many people go through a depression when their children leave home. This happens so often that we even have a name for it; empty nest syndrome.

Viktor Frankl was an Austrian Neurologist and Psychiatrist who found himself in a German concentration camp at Auschwitz and later to Dachau. He was a slave laborer for five months and then moved to a physician's role. After suffering the horrors of the concentration camps for three years, he was liberated and began writing as part of his healing process. He wrote 'Man's Search for Meaning' in 1959. The book demonstrates the importance of understanding the meaning of one's life. Those individuals in the camps that lost their meaning of life (THERE) perished. They gave up. Those who had the why to live (something greater than themselves) could survive the what. Viktor Frankl learned many lessons that he has passed down in his books. He said, "Everyone has his own specific vocation or mission in life; everyone must carry out a concrete assignment that demands fulfillment. Therein he cannot be replaced, nor can his life be repeated, thus, everyone's task is unique as his specific opportunity to implement it."

"Ever more people today have the means to live, but no meaning to live for."—Viktor E. Frankl

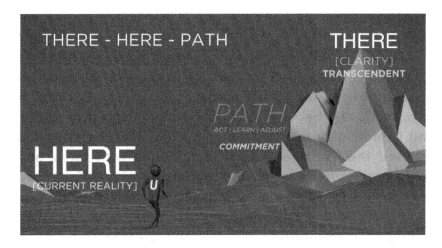

What should a Transcendent THERE look like? How do I know what my purpose in life is? To answer these questions, there are really only two places we can look. This is true with all questions. We can look at what society and culture says our purpose should be or we can look at scripture. We can look at what the society in a world led by Satan says is a good THERE or we can look at what God says is a good THERE. Let's dive into God's word.

Philippians 2: 4-8

Let each of you look out not only for his own interests, but also for the interests of others. Let this mind be in you which was also in Christ Jesus, who, being in the form of God, did not consider it robbery to be equal with God, but made Himself of no reputation, taking the form of a bondservant, *and* coming in the likeness of men. And being found in appearance as a man, He humbled Himself and became obedient to *the point of* death, even the death of the cross.-NKJV

The scripture verse above helps us see what Jesus had for his THERE. Paul is telling us that Jesus' THERE was to obey his father. We can see that his purpose on earth was obedience. Obedience unto death if necessary.

Matthew 25: 14-30

"For *the kingdom of heaven is* like a man traveling to a far country, *who* called his own servants and delivered his goods to them. And to one he gave five talents, to another two, and to another one, to each according to his own ability; and immediately he went on a journey. Then he who had received the five talents went and traded with them, and made another five talents. And likewise he who *had received* two gained two more also. But he who had received one went and dug in the ground, and hid his lord's money. After a long time the lord of those servants came and settled accounts with them.

"So he who had received five talents came and brought five other talents, saying, 'Lord, you delivered to me five talents; look, I have gained five more talents besides them.' His lord said to him, 'Well *done,* good and faithful servant; you were faithful over a few things, I will make you ruler over many things. Enter into the joy of your lord.' He also who had received two talents came and said, 'Lord, you delivered to me two talents; look, I have gained two more talents besides them.' His lord said to him, 'Well *done,* good and faithful servant; you have been faithful over a few things, I will make you ruler over many things. Enter into the joy of your lord.'

"Then he who had received the one talent came and said, 'Lord, I knew you to be a hard man, reaping where you have not sown, and gathering where you have not scattered seed. And I was afraid, and went and hid your talent in the ground. Look, *there* you have *what is* yours.'

"But his lord answered and said to him, 'You wicked and lazy servant, you knew that I reap where I have not sown, and gather where I have not scattered seed. So you ought to have deposited my money with the bankers, and at my coming I would have received back my own with interest.

Therefore take the talent from him, and give *it* to him who has ten talents.

'For to everyone who has, more will be given, and he will have abundance; but from him who does not have, even what he has will be taken away. And cast the unprofitable servant into the outer darkness. There will be weeping and gnashing of teeth.'-NKJV

In the scripture above, Jesus is helping us understand what our THERE should be about. He is telling the disciples that he will be leaving them and he is charging them with a great responsibility. A talent back in the day of Jesus was worth many years' wages. The metaphor here is that just like the servants and the money, the disciples should be investing as well. Not in money but in people. They were to grow his people as the servants were to grow the master's money.

We are charged with this same responsibility to invest in God's people. To carry out the Great Commission. If we follow Jesus' example of obedience and do as he says, we can hear, "Well done, good and faithful servant." To choose not to, as the unprofitable servant did, results in being cast out into the darkness.

Mark 12: 28-31

Then one of the scribes came, and having heard them reasoning together, perceiving that He had answered them well, asked Him, "Which is the first commandment of all?"

Jesus answered him, "The first of all the commandments *is:* 'Hear, O Israel, the LORD our God, the LORD is one. And you shall love the LORD your God with all your heart, with all your soul, with all your mind, and with all your strength.' This *is* the first commandment. And the second, like *it, is* this: 'You shall love your neighbor as yourself.' There is no other commandment greater than these."-NKJV

Matthew 28: 16-20

Then the eleven disciples went to Galilee, to the mountain where Jesus had told them to go. When they saw him, they worshiped him; but some doubted. Then Jesus came to them and said, "All authority in heaven and on earth has been given to me. Therefore go and make disciples of all nations, baptizing them in the name of the Father and of the Son and of the Holy Spirit, and teaching them to obey everything I have commanded you. And surely I am with you always, to the very end of the age."-NKJV

In the passages, Jesus is very clear about what we are to be doing in our lives. We are to love God with all of our being and love our neighbors as ourselves. In loving them, we should be spreading the Gospel. Our Transcendent THERE must then have something to do with obeying God, loving Him above all else and loving our neighbors as ourselves-to hear 'well done good and faithful servant'.

Romans 12: 1-8

I beseech you therefore, brethren, by the mercies of God, that you present your bodies a living sacrifice, holy, acceptable to God, *which is* your reasonable service. And do not be conformed to this world, but be transformed by the renewing of your mind, that you may prove what *is* that good and acceptable and perfect will of God.

Serve God with Spiritual Gifts

For I say, through the grace given to me, to everyone who is among you, not to think *of himself* more highly than he ought to think, but to think soberly, as God has dealt to each one a measure of faith. For as we have many members in one body, but all the members do not have the same function, so we, *being* many, are one body in Christ, and

individually members of one another. Having then gifts differing according to the grace that is given to us, *let us use them*: if prophecy, *let us prophesy* in proportion to our faith; or ministry, *let us use it* in *our* ministering; he who teaches, in teaching; he who exhorts, in exhortation; he who gives, with liberality; he who leads, with diligence; he who shows mercy, with cheerfulness.-NKJ V

In the scripture reading above, Paul is telling us we all have spiritual gifts. He is saying that we should be using those spiritual gifts to serve others. So, if we will follow Jesus' example and obey God, then we will do what he has told us to do by loving God above everything and loving our neighbor as ourselves. We can use our spiritual gifts to serve others and in the end hear, "Well done good and faithful servant."

When we think of relatives or friends who have passed away, we normally don't think about how many cars they had, how much money they made or what their title may have been. Those are simply resume virtues. We usually talk about how they impacted the lives of those around them. These are the eulogy virtues. Our eulogy virtues are the legacy we leave to others.

When I ask groups of people if they know who their father's grandfather was, no one can answer. In two to three generations after you leave this world, statistically no one will remember you or rarely talk about you. However, the life lessons you pass on and the eulogy virtues you help instill in others can change eternity. Not just their eternity but yours as well. When we focus on serving others and helping them down the road of life, we are teaching life lessons that get passed on throughout the generations. These virtues and values help them lead a more Christ-like existence and inevitably change their eternity as they pass along those same virtues and values. While serving others in this capacity, you are doing what Christ asked us to do and therefore also changing your eternity.

Agnes' Story

Agnes was born August 27th 1910 and died Sep 5th 1997. Her tombstone reads 27 Aug 1910-5 Sep 1997.

Like all of us, Agnes was born and, like what will happen with all of us, she died. It's the DASH on her tombstone that we will briefly talk about. Some of the achievements that make up Agnes' dash are the Nobel Peace Prize (which we are all familiar with), the Bharat Rhatna which is the highest civilian award of the Republic of India. The award is conferred "in recognition of exceptional service/performance of the highest order", the Padmashree (4th highest award in India for civilians), the Jawaharla Nehru (international award from India) to name a few. She has an airport named after her, a university, several charitable organizations, a train, and a public holiday in Albania all in her honor.

You see, Agnes knew Christ from a very young age and at 12 years old had made up her mind that she wanted to be a missionary and spread the word of Christ. At age 18 she left her family home in Macedonia and joined a convent in India called the Order of Laretto. There, she taught young children geography and catechism for several years. However, the poverty of India weighed heavy upon her soul so she asked to leave the convent to serve the poor in the slums of Calcutta.

She was sorely tempted during this phase of her life. She had to beg for supplies to aid the poor and she herself lived in extreme poverty. She is quoted as saying during this moment, "Our Lord wants me to be a free nun covered with the poverty of the cross. Today, I learned a good lesson. The poverty of the poor must be so hard for them. While looking for a home I walked and walked till my arms and legs ached. I thought how much they must ache in body and soul, looking for a home, food and health. Then, the comfort of Laretto [her former congregation] came to tempt me. 'You have only to say the word and all that will be yours again,' the Tempter kept on saying. She fought back by saying, "Of free choice, my God, and out of love for you, I desire to remain and do whatever be Your Holy will in my regard. I did not let a single tear come."

In 1950, Agnes petitioned the Vatican to start her own order called the Missionaries of Charity with the mission of looking after those persons who nobody else was prepared to look after. This organization today has more than 4,500 nuns looking after orphanages, AIDs hospices, disabled children, the elderly, homeless, and much more.

Agnes continued her charity work throughout her life. She traveled to many needy places in the world even saving 37 school children caught on the front lines during the height of the siege of Beirut in 1982. She even worked with those inflicted with Leprosy. Her list of accomplishments goes on and on.

You are probably very familiar with Agnes and her life story. You see, Agnes was not always known by her birth name. When she joined the convent at age 18, she was baptized and changed her name. She changed her name to Teresa. She became known as Blessed Teresa of Calcutta and eventually Mother Teresa.

In 2010, 13 years after her death, India released a coin on the anniversary of her birthday to commemorate her and, most recently, Pope Francis has forwarded the canonization process for her to be recognized as a saint.

Mother Teresa's dash on her tombstone is filled with knowing Christ and serving others. What will your dash consist of? What is the objective for your life? And do you have clarity of that objective? Mother Teresa said, "Of free choice, my God, and out of love for you, I desire to remain and do whatever be your Holy will in my regard."

The Five Whys

When trying to decide on what your THERE for life, marriage or children is, it's a good practice to use the "5 whys". This simple exercise was adopted from *The Fifth Discipline* by

Peter Senge. The 5 whys help us better learn the meaning behind our statement. Say I had a THERE to be the CEO of my own company. My first question would be the first why.

1st Why? To have several employees

2nd Why? I want a larger sphere of influence.

3rd Why? I want to be able to provide a place for good people to work and grow.

4th Why? To serve others.

5th Why? Because God told us that to love him I should love others as I love myself.

We have now come to the point of it all. The THERE isn't to be the CEO of a company. It is to serve others through obeying God. Can I do this without being a CEO? Of course I can. I can work on the THERE of serving others and glorifying God every day of my life. Does this mean I should give up my "goal" of being a CEO? Not at all. That is a good goal. But it is not my THERE. Where I am or what title I have cannot stop me from always moving towards my THERE. If I don't complete my goal of being a CEO, I can still find joy in the fact that I can serve others around me and there is nothing that anyone can do to stop that. Becoming a CEO may expand my sphere of influence to serve people on a greater scale but it is not necessary to move towards my THERE. Whether I am at work, church, the gym, the grocery store, home or in the voting booth, I can still focus on my THERE and serve others. If I were to lose my job, quit the gym or lose my home, I can still work towards my THERE. Those other things are just circumstances that I am in as long as I can find other people, I can find a way to serve them. This can come through my personal example, teaching, giving, leading or any number of other ways to impact/influence people.

In my previous example of deployments, if I would have had a good Transcendent THERE of serving others to the glory of God rather than to get everyone home safely, I would have realized what was next. Serving them through their reintegration issues. I could have led by a better personal example of how to overcome the struggles that reintegration throws at you. That example could have possibly made a difference for the men in my command. Instead I was feeling off. I was feeling a little depressed and even unmotivated each time I would come home. What should have been a joyous occasion, became "going through the motions".

Having a great THERE and being committed to it is what made the aforementioned leaders great. Do you have a transcendent THERE? Are you committed to it through personal loss or death if necessary? If so, you have the opportunity to be the hero of your own story. You have the capability to be one of those leaders. Maybe not everyone will know your name but there will be many people that you will influence. They will take those life lessons with them and pass them along. You will have changed eternity; theirs and yours.

It is not what a man does that is of final importance but what he is in what he does. The atmosphere produced by a man, much more than his actions, has lasting influence.

John 13: 12-17

So when He had washed their feet, taken His garments, and sat down again, He said to them, "Do you know what I have done to you? You call Me Teacher and Lord, and you say well, for *so* I am.[4] If I then, *your* Lord and Teacher, have washed your feet, you also ought to wash one another's feet. For I have given you an example, that you should do as I have done to you. Most assuredly, I say to you, a servant is not greater than his master; nor is he who is sent greater than he who sent him. If you know these things, blessed are you if you do them.-NKJV

Having a THERE for our lives helps to create the structural tension for creating the path of least resistance. We begin with the end in mind. Where do I want to be when I stand before the judgment seat of Christ? Our scripture readings tell us that we are supposed to love and obey God above all others. We are to love our neighbors as ourselves and serve them with our spiritual gifts. If we do all these things we are investing in a great treasure and will hear, "Well done, good and faithful servant."

"Don't aim at success. The more you aim at it and make it a target, the more you are going to miss it. For success, like happiness, cannot be pursued; it must ensue, and it only does so as the unintended side effect of one's personal dedication to a cause greater than oneself or as the by-product of one's surrender to a person other than oneself. Happiness must happen, and the same holds for success: you have to let it happen by not caring about it. I want you to listen to what your conscience commands you to do and go on to carry it out to the best of your knowledge. Then you will live to see that in the long-run—in the long-run, I say!—success will follow you precisely because you had forgotten to think about it."—<u>Viktor E. Frankl</u>, <u>Man's Search for Meaning</u>

What is the THERE for your life? What is the THERE for your marriage? What is the THERE for your children? Having a transcendent THERE gives you an eternal perspective through your daily walk in life.

CHAPTER 2

Goal Setting and the Two THEREs

Proverbs 21:5 *"The plans of the diligent lead to profit as surely as haste leads to poverty."*

Goal Setting

Being goal oriented can be very helpful in making progress down the PATH towards your THERE. Research shows that people who set goals are more likely to be successful in life. We call these goals Milestones. These Milestones are not the transcendent THERE we are moving towards, they are just smaller more tangible THEREs that light the PATH towards our transcendent THERE.

These goals/milestones don't take the place of our Transcendent THERE but help us move in that direction. Prior to setting a goal or Milestone, we should determine if it is actually a goal that supports our THERE. Many times we will have an awesome THERE and then put ourselves into cognitive dissonance because we have undermined our THERE by moving off the PATH towards a goal that is not helpful.

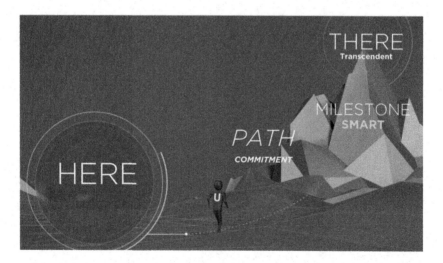

When we set goals we want them to be SMART goals. This format was originally started by George T. Doran in 1981. SMART is an easy acronym to remember that can help us find the clarity we need when setting these goals.

S-Specific: You want your goal/milestone to be specific, clear and free of jargon

M-Measurable: You and others know it was completed (quality, quantity, dollars, etc.)

A-Acceptable or Achievable: Is it in your control or influence to accomplish? Practical, Realistic

R-Results Oriented: Serves the organization's purpose and objective, results not action

T-Time bound: Clear target date or deadline for completion

This acronym is a pretty well-known formula for goal setting. Many people use it but few use it well. It is usually beneficial to have someone listen to your goal to help you be clear on what your goal actually is.

This SMART acronym is excellent for goal setting but cannot be used for your Transcendent THERE. Your Transcendent THERE is not attainable in this life. It is a direction for your life. Therefore, you will never finish it so it can't be time bound and you will never have completed it. It's something you will just keep doing. If your Transcendent THERE is to serve others, it wouldn't be very specific and can therefore be accomplished in many different aspects of our lives. The company I work for has a purpose statement of "Being a self-governed organization that creates asset value using a risk managed investment approach." This is transcendent. We will never get to a point where we are completely self-governed in all aspects of our lives. We will never stop trying to create value and never stop managing risk. It is aspirational and therefore we can't use the SMART acronym for it.

Let's say Ulysses wants to get in better shape. Is that a good goal? No, it doesn't fit the SMART format. However, if Ulysses says, "I want to be able to run one mile in under eight minutes in the next 30 days" that is SMART. Getting in better shape would probably require several SMART goals including diet and goals for cardiorespiratory endurance as well as strength.

Specific-Run one mile in eight minutes in the next 30 days (free of jargon)

Measureable-One mile in eight minutes (he either makes it or he doesn't)

Acceptable/Achievable-based on his current condition, yes.

Results Oriented-Yes it supports his fitness goal.

Time bound-eight minutes and next thirty days.

Accomplishing our goals can be difficult. Research shows that if we make a goal in our minds, we have only about a 20% chance of accomplishing it. If we take the time to write our goals down, our chance of accomplishing the goal goes up to approximately 42%. If we write it down and share it with someone, we have a 62% chance of actually doing it. However, if we write it down, share it with someone and then have them check in on our progress weekly, we get to approximately a 76% chance of accomplishing our goal.

This tells us that if we are setting a goal and really want to achieve it that we should give it the best chance of success we can. We need to write out our goals, share them with others and have an accountability partner who will help us hold ourselves accountable for it. This requires us to have someone in our lives who understands what our THERE is. When we do this for each other, we are serving one another and doing what God asked us to do.

When we have a goal we really want to accomplish, it's going to be very important to not let it become our ultimate focus. We don't want to lose sight of what's important in life. Focusing on our Transcendent THERE will help us prevent this. It will also prevent us from having an oscillating structure between our goals like the family/work example mentioned earlier. How do we prevent these goals from opposing each other? We focus on our Transcendent THERE and that creates structural tension between the two other goals, causing us to take the path of least resistance. When our Transcendent THERE is something about serving others and we communicate that at work and home, it helps our coworkers and families better understand why we are spending time in the other area and it becomes more acceptable.

My wife knows that my THERE is to serve others to the glory of God. If I am running late from work that day, she knows that it probably is due to spending time with someone who needs some coaching for their career or life circumstances. This simple understanding makes the situation more tolerable. The other half of the equation is that when you are spending family time, it's not as much about the quantity of time as it is the quality of time. When we make the most of our time with our family instead of allowing distractions to take over, we can accomplish the family time goal better. When we put away the cell phones, IPads, video games and television to sit down at the table and have dinner, we may find that our quality of time together can make up for a lot of quantity of time together.

The Two THEREs

Now that we understand the framework of leadership (THP) and we know how to set goals to move towards the THERE, we have to understand the two kinds of THEREs. We have a WE THERE and we have a ME THERE. No matter how focused we are on our WE THERE, our transcendent THERE, the ME THERE is always close by.

Even with our great transcendent THERE we can often find ourselves off the PATH. We start heading towards the wrong THERE without even realizing it. The WE THERE is transcendent and about serving others where the ME THERE is self-serving and deceitful. The WE THERE understands that all of us have ingrained in us the desire to be great from our creator. The ME THERE tells us that fulfilling the desire to become great comes through doing for me. **The WE THERE knows that doing what is best for me is doing what is best for others; serving WE.**

This is one of the great paradoxes of life. Doing what is best for me is doing what is best for others. The ME THERE comes from a societal perspective that has become part of our culture. The WE THERE understands that what our society and worldly culture tells us is a lie. Society and culture inundate us with movies, songs, commercials and writings that tell us the things that make us great are money, power, position, sex, control, and material possessions. In Biblical terms we can understand the two THEREs as the Spirit and the Flesh.

We find ourselves drifting towards the flesh when ME gets in the way. We are very susceptible to "keeping up with the Jones's". We all want to be great. We all want to be deemed successful in life. However, what we are told through Hollywood and television is a lie. There is only one truth and it is God's truth. What does scripture say is best for me? What does God say being great is?

Galatians 5: 16-26

I say then: Walk in the Spirit, and you shall not fulfill the lust of the flesh. For the flesh lusts against the Spirit, and the Spirit against the flesh; and these are contrary to one another, so that you do not do the things that you wish. But if you are led by the Spirit, you are not under the law.

Now the works of the flesh are evident, which are: adultery, fornication, uncleanness, lewdness, idolatry, sorcery, hatred, contentions, jealousies, outbursts of wrath, selfish ambitions, dissensions, heresies, envy, murders, drunkenness, revelries, and the like; of which I tell you beforehand, just as I also told *you* in time past, that those who practice such things will not inherit the kingdom of God.

But the fruit of the Spirit is love, joy, peace, longsuffering, kindness, goodness, faithfulness, gentleness, and self-control. Against such there is no law. And those *who are* Christ's have crucified the flesh with its passions and desires. If we live in the Spirit, let us also walk in the Spirit. Let us not become conceited, provoking one another, envying one another.-NKJV

When we examine ourselves in truth and come to our true current reality, we can find several of the words in Paul's writing about the flesh apply to us. Hopefully we can also find something in Paul's writing about the spirit that fits us as well. Paul struggled with the spirit and flesh (the two THEREs) his entire life so it would stand to reason that we will as well.

Even when we know these simple truths, we can suffer from a bit of cognitive dissonance when it comes to the two THEREs. The flesh (ME THERE) just gets a little sneakier and we start to convince ourselves that we are doing what's best for others. Taking the time to examine our motives can help us realize that sometimes when we want to "fix" others to make our lives better we are serving ME instead of WE. Of course, we cannot fix anyone and this rarely helps any situation. However, if we don't think about our motives we will find ourselves going down the PATH towards the ME THERE very quickly.

Where we look, we tend to go. Have you ever seen a car accident on the side of the road? As people check out the accident instead of paying attention to the road, they soon find themselves driving off of it. This is true with the Two THEREs. The one we look at and feed the most is the one that will win. If we spend time in scripture and prayer and serving others more than we do focusing on ME, we will find ourselves walking in the Spirit instead of the Flesh.

Looking back to our story of Chamberlain and the 20th Maine on Little Round Top, it's easy to see the two THEREs present. Chamberlain was faced with the WE THERE of serving the greater mission to his country and his army or serving the ME THERE of self-preservation. He may have even felt the pull from the ME THERE to get off the hill under the premise that he would not be serving himself. He would be serving his men and preventing them from dying in a battle they could not win. After the second charge of the Confederates, there appeared to be no way to absorb the third charge. Leaving the hill would preserve his men. That is the sneakiness of the flesh. It creeps into our hearts and minds and convinces us that we are serving others when we are actually serving ourselves.

Chamberlain decided to serve the greater body of men. He decided to serve the greater army and the greater mission rather than serve the ME THERE. You may not be faced with a life and death decision like Chamberlain today, but every decision you make concerning others is subject to the same level of cognitive dissonance. You know what is in the best interest of the greater good but the ME THERE gets you to second guess things and tries to get you to do things for the wrong reasons and you will justify why you do it in your mind.

Romans 8: 5-9

For those who are according to the flesh set their minds on the things of the flesh, but those who are according to the Spirit, the things of the Spirit. For the mind set on the flesh is death, but the mind set on the Spirit is life and peace, because the mind set on the flesh is hostile toward God; for it does not subject itself to the law of God, for it is not even able to do so, and those who are in the flesh cannot please God. However, you are not in the flesh but in the Spirit, if indeed the Spirit of God dwells in you. But if anyone does not have the Spirit of Christ, he does not belong to Him.-NKJV

Challenge your decisions. Challenge your motives. Ask yourself, "What would God have me do?" Ask, "What does scripture say about this?" Stay away from worrying about what others may say or what others may think. Keep the end in mind and focus on your transcendent THERE.

The two THEREs lie so close together that we often believe we are serving others when in reality we are serving ME. We all desire to be great. God gave us this desire and it is good. The problem does not lie in this desire. The problem lies in our interpretation of what great is. Our society puts value on things like how much money we have. If I am rich, I am successful and that makes me great. Society tells us that if I am famous I am successful and that makes me great. Society tell us that if we own a large house, multiple cars or have numerous sexual partners we are successful and that makes us great. This is the lie that Satan has been using against us for all time. The resume virtues are not what is important in this life or the next. Our eulogy virtues are what make us great.

I think we can say there are three ways to become great and all of them are moving towards the WE THERE and not the ME THERE. The first is to create something great that serves others. This could be a great work of art like Michelangelo or a great invention life Da Vinci. It could be an advance in medical technology like Louis Pasteur whose discoveries of the principles of vaccination, microbial fermentation and pasteurization have saved countless lives. All of these demonstrate a level of greatness.

The second way to become great is by experiencing something or encountering someone; in other words greatness can be found not only in a work but through love of another. Love is pursuing the best for others patiently, kindly, sacrificially and unconditionally. This is God's perfect love for us. I have seen this kind of love from a man I will call Staff Sergeant (SSG) Murray.

SSG Murray's Story

Afghanistan is one of the most heavily land mined countries in the world. There seems to be about as many land mines as there are people. Early in 2002, SSG Murray was leading a dismounted patrol of 12 men through some mountains near his outpost in the Eastern Paktika Province of Afghanistan. The elevation, heat and heavy load that we carried would slowly start to take its toll and wear you out by about mid-day. It was right around that time that SSG Murray stepped on a buried anti-personnel landmine. The explosion knocked him to the ground and cleaved his right leg from his body. The other men nearest him were spread out enough that they were spared injury from the explosion. SSG Murray, mercifully, immediately lost consciousness. His men immediately performed first aid and tied a tourniquet around what was left of his leg above the knee. When they were able to extricate him from the mine field and get him back to our aid station he regained consciousness. When he woke up, the first thing he said was, "how are my men?" He did not ask about his leg. He did not ask if he was going to live. He knew something bad had happened and wasn't sure what had happened after he stepped on the mine. He asked about his men. His love for the men he served was never more prevalent than at that moment. This unselfish concern for others over himself demonstrated his greatness. Anytime someone puts the best for others above themselves they demonstrate this love and can easily be seen as great.

The third and most important way that we find greatness is through overcoming suffering or through sacrifice for others. However, this is not about suffering for suffering's sake. This is about perspective and perseverance. We all have a level of suffering that we go through in our lives. We all deal with levels of adversity. What is difficult for some is not as difficult for others. It is how we look at it that matters. When things don't go our way, we can look at it in only two ways. We can look at it through the lens of a victim, pity ourselves and blame others or we can look at it through the lens of choice. We can choose to see the positive outcomes that we can achieve from overcoming adversity. Armed with this perspective, when things go poorly in our lives, good. Rejoice. It's another opportunity to be closer to God. It's an opportunity to learn something new about yourself. It's an opportunity to show others how to be resilient in the face of the storm. It's an opportunity to discover the greatness within yourself and teach others how to do the same through your example.

We can see this through a historical example of Washington at Valley Forge.

Washington at Valley Forge

At the end of 1777 the Revolutionary Army camped out at Valley Forge. It was a terrible time. The army had eight days of supplies when they went to ground for the entire winter. They had just come off of two major battlefield losses. Morale was the lowest it would ever be. There was no food and men were literally freezing to death.

Many of the senior officers left for home while the enlisted men were forced to live in unfathomable conditions for the winter. It was the privilege of being an officer at that time. You just had to come back for the fighting season. However, one senior leader stayed on. One man continued to walk through the camps every evening and encourage his men. George Washington stayed and suffered with his men. He set an example through his personal leadership. It was as if his personal will was the only thing that held the army together. Most of the men looked to Washington as a father figure.

He was physically, mentally, spiritually and financially everything his men wanted to be. He was old enough to be the father of most of them and they looked up to him. He was a great man because he chose to suffer with his men who would rather perish than let him down. Let me say that again... they would rather die than let him down! He did all he could to bring in supplies for his men. Finally, an Iroquois war chief who had befriended Washington years before snuck through enemy lines and returned with his men and over 600 bushels of corn. This saved the army and prevented an early end to the war. From there, Washington was able to bring in a Prussian General, Baron Friedrich Von Steuben. Von Steuben was a professional soldier who understood how to train others. He spent the winter training the militia and when they came out of Valley Forge, they were at last a professional army that could stand toe to toe with the British. Washington's influence had saved the army. This is part of who he was and how he did life.

So, three ways to achieve greatness: Doing great works or deeds, through love of others and through suffering. We can find people that we know and those throughout history that we would say are great who did just one of those. However, we have the greatest example of all three in Jesus Christ. Jesus Christ who performed miracles of healing or feeding the multitude. Jesus Christ who loved others beyond our understanding and Jesus Christ who suffered for us on the cross. Jesus Christ who overcame sin and overcame death through unjustified suffering.

So, the path to greatness is pursuing Christ. It is following his example of service to descend into greatness. To become the servant of others. Through him all things are possible and when we follow him we are leading others...we are serving others.

We can develop structures to help us stay on track and help us avoid the ME THERE. Structure demands behavior. When we have a structure in place, it can help us think of things differently. In the picture below, the red triangle is a typical hierarchy of an oil company and this is true for most organizations. At the top you have a CEO and then there are several layers of executives and managers until you get to the bottom of the of the pyramid structure. This physical structure of how a company works usually demands a behavior that results in everyone from the bottom of the pyramid has to serve or suck up to the people above them. This is a typical mechanistic structure to support the chain of command and communication. However, we can have a mental structure of the organization as shown with the green triangle. This is where our leaders understand that their job is not to lord over those below them in the pyramid but to serve them by placing their needs above their own. This mental structure results in servant leadership.

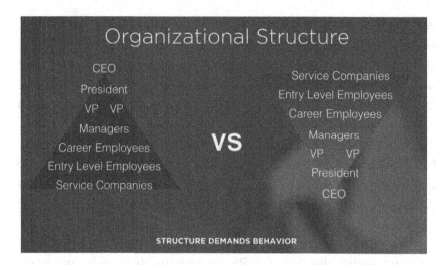

This simple mental model can help us remember to treat others with the same mercy and grace that we desire for ourselves. One day we will all be judged by the same measuring stick we used to judge others. Pope Francis has announced that the Catholic Church's new structure would be the same as our green upside down pyramid in the picture above...Servant Leadership.

We can also put other structures in place to help us stay in the spirit instead of the flesh. It could be going to church or being part of a community group or a Bible study. Maybe it's listening to the Christian music station instead of others. Anything you can do to defend yourself against what society and culture in our country tells you is right over what God and scripture tells you is right would be beneficial.

"A man who becomes conscious of the responsibility he bears toward a human being who affectionately waits for him, or to an unfinished work, will never be able to throw away his life. He knows the "why" for his existence, and will be able to bear almost any "how"."—Viktor E. Frankl, Man's Search for Meaning

CHAPTER 3

Power/Influence and Leadership Styles

(HERE Tool #1)

Power or influence is all in the perception of the person being influenced. If someone believes you have some influence with them, then you have a degree of influence with them. If they don't recognize that power structure in you, you will not have it.

Now that we understand our THERE and how to create one, the next step is to understand our HERE. The HERE is just another word for current reality. It helps us identify our strengths and weakness so that we can better influence others to get THERE (servant leadership). When we know our strengths, we can lean into them to help us influence others and serve them. When we know our weaknesses, we can shore them up or work on them towards self-improvement. We can demonstrate to others a willingness to work on our shortcomings and influence others through our efforts.

Understanding our HERE can be very difficult. We typically think we are further down the PATH than we actually are. We generally have an inflated opinion of ourselves that can cause us to not have an accurate assessment of our strengths and weaknesses. We want to know the truth of where we are. Only God knows the truth. However, to help us dial in a little closer to our current reality, we can try to look at ourselves objectively. Next, we can get others' opinion of where they think we are. Typically the truth is somewhere in between our own opinion and theirs.

Throughout the rest of this book I will lay out seven HERE tools to help us better assess our current reality. The first HERE tool is power and leadership styles. The word power can have negative connotations with some people but I will use it interchangeably with influence. There are five types of power or influence that we have with others. Before we dive into them let's look at people in our lives that have had influence with us.

Who was your role model growing up? Who is your role model now? That person had or has a tremendous amount of influence with you. When I ask that question in group settings, I usually hear things like a parent, a teacher or coach, Jesus or even a sports figure.

In a study by Steven H. White and Joseph E. O'Brien, they posed three questions about role models to approximately 830 K-12 students in eastern Kansas. They gave a written survey to the 3rd-12th grade students and interviewed K-2nd grade students. The sequence of questions was arranged so that students were required to consider what a role model was and what they might need to do to become one before identifying who was one of their role models. Once they identified a role model, they were asked to explain why the person or character was a role model to them.

Question one: What is a Role Model?

Overall, responses to this question fell into three categories. The majority of students gave definitions that were general, such as "a role model is someone to look up to" or someone "you want to be like." The second most popular response described a role model as someone who "sets an example" or "does good things." A third category consisted of responses such as someone "who inspires you," "who teaches you," and who "helps you." While related, each set of responses seemed distinct. Respondents seemed influenced by a role model's actions and portrayed role models as a positive or influential person.

Question 2: Who are Your Personal Role Models? Who are these positive or influential people?

Parents and other family members were identified most often as a role model. Teachers were second. Third came popular persons such as sports figures, actors, and musicians. The remaining role models represented less than 8% of the responses and included such figures as God, Martin Luther King, Jr. and "myself."

From this we can understand that parents and teachers are in the top two categories of what children look at as role models. This does change as we go through life. Other people influence us as we move down the PATH. As we get older, we typically look at the best we see in people and want to be like them in that aspect. Some people will have much more influence with us than others. What gives them this influence?

If servant leadership is influencing others to get THERE, we should be trying to gain influence with others to better serve them. This is the key to serving others. Gaining influence to serve them better. As stated earlier, there are five types of influence or power.

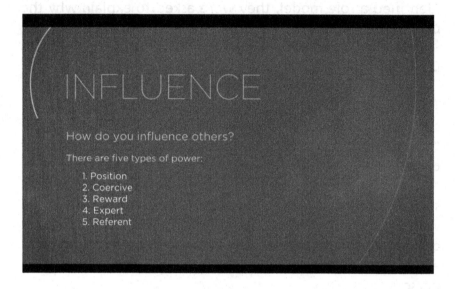

Position Power

The first type of power is Position Power. Position Power is influence based on a position someone holds. This could be a manager at work, a parent, an elected official, a law enforcement professional or a firefighter. If you believe your manager has the power to terminate your employment or give you a pay raise, they have a degree of power over you. If a fireman burst through your door right now and told you to get out of the building or a police officer asks you to exit your vehicle, you are probably going to follow their directions. This is position power. You can gain position power by being placed in positions of greater responsibility.

Coercive Power

The second type of power is Coercive Power. Coercive Power is influence that comes from someone's perception that you have the ability to punish them. If a child believes that a parent has the power to ground them or take away an allowance, then that parent has coercive power with that child. Coercive Power is tied in with Position Power very closely but only represents the ability to punish or take away. We can lose coercive power by not following through with our threats. When you tell little Johnny that he will receive a punishment for not cleaning his room and he doesn't do it, if you don't execute the punishment, you are giving up coercive power. Little Johnny will start to believe that you will not punish him after a few repetitions of this cycle.

You can gain more Coercive Power by following through with what you say you will do. This type of power is often over used. Overuse can also lead to a loss of influence. When we only use coercive power, people become numb to it. You see this with leaders who yell all the time. It becomes ineffective and demoralizing. Unfortunately, many times a novice leader will often fall back on this type of influence because they feel more in control. In these situations, peers and senior leaders should step in and help before that junior leader loses his influence completely.

Reward Power

The third type of power is Reward Power. Reward power is the opposite of Coercive Power but in many ways the same. When you tell someone they will receive a reward for completing a task and then follow through with the reward, you will gain more reward power. If you don't follow through, you will be giving Reward Power away. This power can also be over used. When you constantly give praise for things that

43

just meet the standard, it can become meaningless. We should praise people for doing praiseworthy things. Whenever we do praise, we want it to be true, specific and personal. We should praise in public to reinforce good behavior to others.

Expert Power

The fourth type of power is Expert Power. This power comes from demonstrating a level of expertise in an area that is greater than what the observer possesses. Have you ever been placed onto a team where there is someone who has been on the project for several years? When you look at that person, they have a lot of expert power because they know the material so well. They are who you would approach to ask questions. You may have expert power over others in some areas and not in others.

You can gain expert power by demonstrating proficiency in a task or a subject. You can lose expert power by pretending you know the answer to something when you don't. In those instances you quickly lose credibility. We can help our subordinates gain expert power by having them teach classes or do presentations. It is important to set them up for success when doing this. Have them rehearse with you so they do a good job. If they do poorly, we have set them up to lose credibility and they have given away their expert power. Research shows that mastering a task takes 10,000 hours of focused effort. For instance, to be a world-class pianist you would need to put in 10,000 hours of focused effort once you have the basics. How much daily effort do you put into being a master of your profession? Is it focused effort? This effort results in a high degree of Expert Power; but we have some Expert Power over others who have fewer focused hours than we do. To better influence others to get THERE, we should put effort into becoming a subject matter expert in our professions or other areas of our lives.

Referent Power

The fifth power type is the most influential. It is Referent Power. This type of power comes from doing life right. Have you ever had anyone come up to you and ask, "What's different about you?" When we live life the way God intended us to, it is very attractive to others. People want to be like you. Earlier, you were asked who your role model in life was. That person had a lot of referent power with you. You wanted to exemplify their behavior or a portion of it. Do you have this power with someone else? It is very influential and when you wield a great deal of referent power you have to be careful how you use it. A great deal of referent power coupled with coercive power can be devastating. A great deal of referent power coupled with reward power can put someone on cloud nine and potentially create a foster dependency of needing continuous positive reinforcement from the role model.

You can give your referent power away through inappropriate actions or statements. If you choose to live life outside of what God intended, you will lose that influence with others. You can gain more referent power by strengthening your pillars (Tenets of Referent Power).

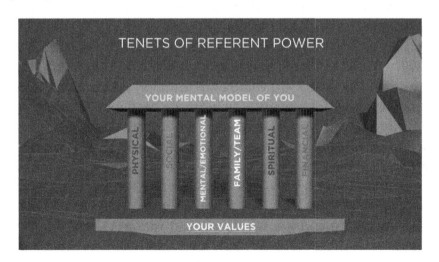

The Tenets of Referent Power are based on the Comprehensive Fitness that the Army uses to help soldiers deal with adversity. Some of the pillars depicted here are a bit different than what you would find in the Comprehensive Fitness model.

Foundational to referent power is our values. When we think of those who had a lot of referent power with us, it is because we saw that they had good values. Before looking at each pillar individually, let's examine our values. What do you value? This is a very important question to better understand our HERE. What we value is extremely important to having a truthful understanding of our current reality. Take a moment and contemplate the question of what your values are. Write down your top five values.

When I ask the question of what your top five values are in a group setting, almost everyone will have written down a value like integrity, honesty, candor or truth. You probably had one of those words on your list. After asking the question of who had one of those words on their list, I typically dive into what that means. Do you share truth with others? Do you tell someone when they are not performing to standard? Do you give others honest feedback? The answer statistically is simply, no. Sharing truth with others is a value that we all know we should have but few actually do.

This is what makes understanding our HERE so difficult. I will go back to the question of what do you value? The question is what do you value and not what should you value. Look at your list again and really take a hard look at yourself. How do you know what you value? A good litmus test for this is where you spend your time and where you spend your money. Do you spend your time at work? Do you spend your time looking at pornography? Do you spend your time drinking, playing video games or using drugs? Look at your checkbook and see where you are spending your money. These are the things you value the most. Having an honest assessment of your current reality is very difficult and the reason why we don't have a good assessment of our HERE. We generally are not even honest with ourselves, let alone others.

Let's take a new look at our values. What do you value? Where do you spend your time and money? The "five whys" can help us here as well. If you spend most of your time at work, why? Is it because you don't like your family or is it because you are serving them? Ask the five whys to get to the real reason you are at work or why you are spending your time or money doing certain things. Understand your HERE through objective personal examination. Once you have done this, you will better understand the foundation for your pillars. You will better understand why you have so much influence or so little. You will better understand your HERE. The wise man builds his house upon the rock while the foolish man builds his house upon the sand.

In the picture of referent power, the depiction of you as a house with a foundation and supported by pillars is very simplified but is a great mental model to have when thinking of comprehensive fitness. When we have weak values, it can be catastrophic for us because our entire existence can fall apart. If we have a weak pillar, the other pillars must be strong enough to support us. For example, if you have a physical ailment or obesity it can cause you to have social issues, mental/emotional issues, financial issues from buying the next great diet pill, and even issues with your family and God. If your other pillars are strong enough, you can continue to stand and operate normally. If your other pillars are already cracked or weak, they could also collapse and cause you to spiral down into depression and sometimes worse. This model is used to teach resiliency. It is meant to help people understand that all of these categories are important and intertwined, more like a braid of rope than separate pillars. We need to work on our pillars to keep them strong so we are ready when adversity hits.

Physical Pillar

The first pillar that we talk about is the physical pillar. This is first because when you meet someone for the first time you are sizing them up based on physical appearance and presence. This happens in the first two tenths of a second. Are they tall, handsome or pretty, have a strong jaw line, short, tubby, and do they look like me? This is all done subconsciously and automatically. We normally predicate our future relationship with that person based on that initial impression of how they appear.

This pillar includes how someone represents themselves. Are they in shape? Are they on time? Do they work hard? Do they look the part? Do they look professional? This may sound shallow and sad but it is a fact. We almost always vote for the taller candidate in a presidential election. We tend to give less credibility to people who don't show up on time.

There has been a lot of research done on the benefits of physical fitness. This research shows us that the more physically fit we are, the more capable we are of handling stress, being confident in ourselves, getting hurt less and recovering more quickly from injury. We look up to people who have a greater physical presence. We see this for both men and women. Men will many times have a professional athlete as the person who they use as a role model. The physical pillar is so predominate that they infer the rest of the pillars. However, professional athletes may have a very strong physical pillar and not have any other strong pillars. We see this especially with their financial pillars. 79% of NBA players and 75% of NFL players will file bankruptcy. Women will also infer strong pillars with a commanding physical presence. They subconsciously tend to look at a taller man as someone who will be more capable of providing them security and are therefore more attracted to the "tall, dark and handsome" stereotype.

Social Pillar

The second pillar is the Social Pillar. Once you meet someone for the first time and have made an initial assessment based on the physical pillar, we begin to communicate. You will very quickly be able to assess whether that person is introverted or extroverted. Do they have interpersonal skills or are they socially awkward? If we have a strong social pillar, we typically have deep meaningful relationships with many people. We have a strong social network of friends. We can see the necessity of this when we are having difficult times. Do you have a social network you can rely on? With the advent of the recent technological advances, young people have many more social relationships but they are typically through social media, online game play or text messaging. They don't have the deeper relationships that provide comfort and support when we are in need. If we determine our HERE as having a weak social pillar we can set some SMART goals to work on it.

Mental/Emotional Pillar

The third pillar is the Mental/Emotional Pillar. After meeting someone and sizing them up physically and socially, we can very quickly determine whether or not they are well read, intelligent, and in good control of their emotions. Do you make it a priority to read? Are you in good control of your emotions or do people have to be careful what they say around you for fear of offending you or making you angry? We have all been around people that and we feel we have to walk on egg shells. These people have a weak Mental/Emotional Pillar. This pillar consists of your Intelligence Quotient (IQ) and your Emotional Quotient (EQ). People can be physically an adult but have very poor self-awareness and be an emotional child or adolescent. Having a clear understanding of your current reality (HERE) will help you identify any shortcomings or strengths of this pillar to work on with your SMART goals.

Family/Team Pillar

The fourth pillar is the Family/Team Pillar. Once you get to know someone a little more than the initial conversation, you begin to see how they treat the people around them. Do they serve others or expect to be served? Are they a good parent, sibling, child or spouse? Do they treat others with respect? When we think about referent power and who we want to be like, this pillar can be very important. We all know people who don't treat their families or team the way they should.

Spiritual Pillar

The fifth pillar is the Spiritual pillar. As Christians, we understand this pillar as the thread that holds all the others together. Do we have a good relationship with God? This pillar is possibly the easiest and most difficult for us to work on. We are as close to God as we choose to be. What prevents us from being close to him and having a fulfilling relationship with our creator is the ME THERE. Your relationship with your creator will ultimately determine the fulfillment you find in life. Knowing that when we are experiencing challenges in life, we are going through them for a reason is an important perspective.

Financial Pillar

The final pillar is the Financial Pillar. Do you handle your finances or do your finances handle you? Are you a good steward of God's resources? Learning to handle our finances well is Biblical. When we manage money well and have a strong financial pillar that includes an emergency fund, when difficulties hit, we are more capable of handling them without finding ourselves in debt and stressed out about how we will make ends meet. Do you have money left at the end of the month or month left at the end of your money?

All of these pillars will give you the referent power or influence to be able to serve others. This is the best way to lead by example. Be a role model for doing life right. Pour energy into your pillars and you will attract others and be able to influence them to serve others. You will be an example of how to handle adversity and influence others through your actions. If you aren't putting energy into your pillars and values, energy is leaving them. This is the law of entropy. Everything in life undergoes entropy. This law simply states that if you are not adding energy to something, it is undergoing decay, corrosion or descending back to disorder and chaos. The easiest example for this is the physical pillar. After a total muscle failure workout, it takes 48 hours for the muscle to recover. By 72 hours, that muscle has completely recovered. By 96 hours, the muscle begins to atrophy. The same is true with all of our values and pillars. If we don't put energy into them, energy is leaving them.

Which pillar is your strongest? Which pillar do you need to work on the most? Having a clear understanding of these questions and your values will give you a much more clear understanding of your current reality; your HERE.

To better illustrate how the pillars work, let's look at what God shows us through the life of Job.

Job 1-2:

There was a man in the land of Uz, whose name *was* Job; and that man was blameless and upright, and one who feared God and shunned evil. And seven sons and three daughters were born to him. Also, his possessions were seven thousand sheep, three thousand camels, five hundred yoke of oxen,

five hundred female donkeys, and a very large household, so that this man was the greatest of all the people of the East.

And his sons would go and feast *in their* houses, each on his *appointed* day, and would send and invite their three sisters to eat and drink with them. So it was, when the days of feasting had run their course that Job would send and sanctify them, and he would rise early in the morning and offer burnt offerings *according to* the number of them all. For Job said, "It may be that my sons have sinned and cursed God in their hearts." Thus Job did regularly.

Now there was a day when the sons of God came to present themselves before the Lord, and Satan also came among them. And the Lord said to Satan, "From where do you come?"

So Satan answered the Lord and said, "From going to and fro on the earth, and from walking back and forth on it."

Then the Lord said to Satan, "Have you considered My servant Job, that *there is* none like him on the earth, a blameless and upright man, one who fears God and shuns evil?"

So Satan answered the Lord and said, "Does Job fear God for nothing? Have You not made a hedge around him, around his household, and around all that he has on every side? You have blessed the work of his hands, and his possessions have increased in the land. But now, stretch out Your hand and touch all that he has, and he will surely curse You to Your face!"

And the Lord said to Satan, "Behold, all that he has *is* in your power; only do not lay a hand on his *person*."

So Satan went out from the presence of the Lord.

Now there was a day when his sons and daughters *were* eating and drinking wine in their oldest brother's house; and a messenger came to Job and said, "The oxen were plowing and the donkeys feeding beside them, when the Sabeans raided *them* and took them away—indeed they have killed the servants with the edge of the sword; and I alone have escaped to tell you!"

While he *was* still speaking, another also came and said, "The fire of God fell from heaven and burned up the sheep and the servants, and consumed them; and I alone have escaped to tell you!"

While he *was* still speaking, another also came and said, "The Chaldeans formed three bands, raided the camels and took them away, yes, and killed the servants with the edge of the sword; and I alone have escaped to tell you!"

While he *was* still speaking, another also came and said, "Your sons and daughters *were* eating and drinking wine in their oldest brother's house, and suddenly a great wind came from across the wilderness and struck the four corners of the house, and it fell on the young people, and they are dead; and I alone have escaped to tell you!"

Then Job arose, tore his robe, and shaved his head; and he fell to the ground and worshiped. And he said, "Naked I came from my mother's womb, and naked shall I return there. The LORD gave, and the LORD has taken away; Blessed be the name of the LORD." In all this Job did not sin nor charge God with wrong.

Again there was a day when the sons of God came to present themselves before the LORD, and Satan came also among them to present himself before the LORD. ² And the LORD said to Satan, "From where do you come?"

Satan answered the LORD and said, "From going to and fro on the earth, and from walking back and forth on it."

Then the LORD said to Satan, "Have you considered My servant Job, that *there is* none like him on the earth, a blameless and upright man, one who fears God and shuns evil? And still he holds fast to his integrity, although you incited Me against him, to destroy him without cause."

So Satan answered the LORD and said, "Skin for skin! Yes, all that a man has he will give for his life. But stretch out

Your hand now, and touch his bone and his flesh, and he will surely curse You to Your face!"

And the Lord said to Satan, "Behold, he *is* in your hand, but spare his life."

So Satan went out from the presence of the Lord, and struck Job with painful boils from the sole of his foot to the crown of his head. And he took for himself a potsherd with which to scrape himself while he sat in the midst of the ashes.

Then his wife said to him, "Do you still hold fast to your integrity? Curse God and die!"

But he said to her, "You speak as one of the foolish women speaks. Shall we indeed accept good from God, and shall we not accept adversity?" In all this Job did not sin with his lips.

Now when Job's three friends heard of all this adversity that had come upon him, each one came from his own place—Eliphaz the Temanite, Bildad the Shuhite, and Zophar the Naamathite. For they had made an appointment together to come and mourn with him, and to comfort him. And when they raised their eyes from afar, and did not recognize him, they lifted their voices and wept; and each one tore his robe and sprinkled dust on his head toward heaven. So they sat down with him on the ground seven days and seven nights, and no one spoke a word to him, for they saw that *his* grief was very great.

This passage is an excellent way for God to show us how to deal with adversity. We can see that Job had everything taken from him. His health was attacked, his friends mocked him, he was mentally and emotionally anguished, his own wife turned on him and he lost is children, and all of his wealth was stripped from him. He lost all of his pillars with the exception of one. His spiritual pillar sustained him. His faith that God was in control and God knew best sustained Job through losing all of his other pillars.

How would you do in Job's situation? Could you continue to have faith when faced with the level of adversity Job was?

The point is that when all of our pillars are strong, we will better be able to handle adversity when it strikes; not if, but when. If you found out you had contracted a horrible disease, your physical pillar would start to crack. That means that the rest of your pillars and your values would need to sustain you. They would definitely feel the burden of the cracks in the physical pillar but if you had an emergency fund to deal with things like this, your finances would be fine. If you had a strong relationship with your family and team, you would have people surrounding you that could help. If you were mentally and emotionally strong, you would be better prepared to deal with the issue. If your faith in God was strong enough, you would look at your disease as an opportunity to be closer to God rather than driving you away from him.

A couple of years ago, I had the privilege of hearing Bob Bledsoe speak. Bob was in his mid-eighties and was telling a story about his time with cancer. He was reflecting back on what that horrible disease was doing in his life. However, Bob looked at his time with cancer as a blessing. He stated that he wouldn't change his time with cancer for anything in the world. It was during this time that his relationship with God was the strongest. He recognized that this physical disease was actually a blessing to him. His perspective and faith were a tremendous example to everyone who knew him.

Bob became a personal hero of mine when I heard him speak on this. He had a bit of a Job experience and chose to look at the positive side of it. He faced adversity and chose to be strong. His other pillars were all in place and sustained him. However, it was his spiritual pillar that actually sustained him the most...Not just sustained him but grew ever stronger.

How prepared are you for adversity? Are you ready to demonstrate to others what it means to be resilient? All of these pillars and values are what give you the most influential type of power or influence with others. When people want to be like you, you have an opportunity to better serve them. Let's look at referent power from a historical perspective.

REFERENT POWER-The Newburg Address

In March of 1783, the Revolutionary War was all but over. The last British forces would leave America in September of that year. There was no more fighting and both sides were just waiting for a few more documents to be agreed upon and signed.

Many of the Army's senior officers were disgruntled with the Continental Congress. They had not received their pay, back pay or pensions that they had been promised. This came to a head on March 10th of 1783 at Newburg, New York. The officers decided to meet to determine how they would march the army out into the frontier and give the country back to the British. They scheduled a meeting for the 10th of March.

General George Washington heard about the scheduled meeting and ordered it postponed to March 15th. He spent the next five days speaking with friends searching for advice, praying to God to give him strength and wisdom and writing the most impassioned speech he could come up with. He had also received a speech to read from Congressman Joseph Jones.

The officers began their meeting and had all agreed that the Continental Congress had wronged them. They had not followed through on their promises and it was time to turn everything back over to the King of England. Unnoticed, Washington slid through the side door and upon hearing his disgruntled men he took to the front of the room to read his speech.

*Depiction of Washington by John Trumbull

General Washington gave his very impassioned speech but it met with a great deal of resistance. He talked about loyalty, duty and honor to which the officers very vocally stated that congress had no such honor or loyalty so why should they? Washington's speech had fallen flat and he knew it was over. Everything they had fought for was coming to an end. He was defeated.

Washington had promised Congressman Jones that he would read the speech Jones had written. Defeated, Washington pulled the speech from his pocket and began to read. He stumbled over the first few words as he was emotional and could not read them well without his spectacles. He pulled his spectacles from his pocket and said, "Gentlemen, you will have to forgive me. I have grown gray in your service and now find myself growing blind."

The incident was so moving and powerful that many of the men openly wept. The man who they all wanted to be like and had suffered through every hardship with was not quitting on them. He was still loyal to the cause and had sacrificed as much if not more than any of them. He was still committed to the THERE. Just like that, the insurrection ended. They realized there was something greater than themselves at stake. Through George Washington's act of humility and frailty, they were able to see the WE THERE and were ashamed to have walked towards the ME THERE.

The next day the officers gathered together again and signed a petition commending General Washington for his service and loyalty to the country.

George Washington had a tremendous amount of referent power over his men. He was the man they all aspired to be. He was physically imposing at over six feet. The average height for a man back then was five foot six inches. To add to his physical size, he looked the part of commander in chief. He was always on time and was a veteran who had fought many battles in the French and Indian War. George Washington had great social skills. He was known for his interpersonal skills and ability to communicate well. He treated others with dignity and respect. He was very intelligent and in strong control of his emotions. George Washington was also known for how pious he was. We have all seen the painting of him kneeling next to his horse and praying in the moonlight. He was also very wealthy. He had all of his pillars in order and had great foundational values. He used all of this to influence others on numerous occasions in order to keep our country alive.

It has been said that the only real difference between you now and you five years from now is what you have read and who you have met. This statement would reinforce our Mental and Social Pillars but misses the others. The difference between you today and five years from now is the choices you make to reinforce and strengthen all of your pillars.

When you have all of your pillars in order and continuously put energy into them and our values, people want to be like you. They will look to you for leadership. You will grow your sphere of influence and be more capable of serving others. If you have a THERE that includes serving others, this is how you begin. You start by leading by example. You start by leading yourself. Living life with great values and strong pillars will draw people to you. They will make statements like, "There's something different about you. What is it?" This can lead to great opportunities and transformational leadership.

Leadership Styles

With the understanding that our HERE is heavily influenced by the types of power we wield, it is important to understand how to utilize it. There are five styles or approaches to leadership. They are Directive, Transactional, Participative, Delegative and Transformational.

The first leadership style is Directive. Directive Leadership is the least developmental of the five styles. It is assigning the There-Here-Path to others. There can be appropriate situations to be Directive. You would want to use Directive Leadership when safety is involved, you are dealing with a child, dealing with someone who is immature or time is of the essence. Directive Leadership is based mostly on Position Power.

The second leadership style is Transactional. Transactional Leadership is just like the word sounds. If you do an assigned task, you will get something in return and if you don't do the task there will be some consequence involved. This style of leadership is where most people reside and rarely ever move away from it. Transactional leadership is based on Position, Reward and Coercive Power. We rarely move past this because this is how we are raised. We teach our children from the youngest age that if they do what we ask them to do, they will be rewarded and if they do not, they will be punished. If Little Johnny cleans his room, he will get a cookie, if he doesn't he will be grounded. This pattern of WIFM (What's In It For Me?) continues into the school years where we learn the minimum we have to do to get an A on our assignment. If I show up, do the minimum it takes to get the grade I want, then I can move on and eventually graduate. It then continues into adulthood where we show up to work, do the minimum expected of us to get our paycheck and keep our job. This is a completely transactional lifestyle. I'm not suggesting people should go to work without expecting a paycheck. However, there is more than just doing the minimum for what is expected. This leadership style is good for young people and new employees who have gone through life this way. It is good to help build habits and move people towards something more transformational. When done temporarily with a purpose like building good habits to move people towards Transformational Leadership, it can be very developmental.

You can see this with goal setting. In the company I work for, we do quarterly goals that are tied to a bonus. The goals laid out are SMART goals and the employee will get a percentage of the overall bonus amount based on what percentage of his goals he completes. When we first start doing goals with an employee, they are pretty simple goals. The first few sessions are really just to help them learn to become goal oriented and the biggest reason people will accomplish the goal is simply for the money. It is a very transactional process. After a few goals sessions, the employee usually independently starts to create goals that are much more advanced and will not want to get paid for the simple goals. Usually they will say something like, "I don't want to make that a goal I get paid for because I should be doing that anyways." This is where we really try to encourage them to make goals through others. They will set goals to help someone else accomplish something. This demonstrates they are moving beyond the transactional component of what's in it for me and learn to serve others. This becomes transformational in the lives of both employees and for the company.

The third style of leadership is Participative Leadership. Participative Leadership relies on a lot of Expert Power. This is the on the job training where someone shows you the There-Here-Path. This leadership style is very influential and is good for people who are new to the organization. It is very effective for teaching and mentoring. Participative Leadership can really help to motivate others. When the boss gets out there and helps out, it is extremely motivational for others to see that he is not above any type of work.

The fourth leadership style is Delegative. This leadership style relies on Position, Reward, Coercive and Expert Power. This style is where the leader assigns the THERE and others being delegated to find the PATH. The Delegative style is often the most misunderstood. Many leaders believe that if they just tell others what to do, they are good at delegating. This, however, is not delegating. This is Directing. You can delegate authority but not responsibility. When delegating, the leader is still responsible and must have a structure in place to spot check the project. Those who tell others what to do and then, when it is not done incorrectly, blame the subordinate are just "passing the buck." When done correctly, this leadership approach is very effective and very developmental. This is especially true when those being delegated to feel that it is acceptable to make mistakes and learn from them. As long as the environment is seen as a safe place to fail, subordinates will feel free to make decisions on their own. When any mistake or failure is not seen as a learning opportunity, it will probably cause the person being delegated to feel a great deal of angst and actually cause them to be decision paralyzed. Leaders must also be careful not to spot check too often as this could lead to the perception of micromanagement. When people feel like they are getting micromanaged, it is very demoralizing. We need to feel like we are trusted to make decisions on our own.

The final leadership style is the most developmental. Transformational Leadership can happen when there is a shared There-Here-Path. This means there is a clear THERE communicated sufficiently to create a shared vision. There must also be a common understanding of the current reality (HERE) shared with transparency. Finally there must be commitment to the THERE while traversing the Path, resulting in a learning organization through the Act/Learn/Adjust (ALA) process. Transformational Leadership relies heavily upon Referent Power. This style of leadership is where subordinates try to do what is right simply because it is right and not only for what they may get in return. Have you ever done something for someone when there is no way they could ever possibly repay you? When we serve others without expecting repayment, it is transformational; for them and for you. You are changing their lives and yours. The feeling of fulfillment we get from this can become addicting. We will want to do it more and more. When you go to work and do a great job, beyond what is expected, we get the same feeling. When we do what is right because it is right and not for WIFM, we end up being rewarded with a great sense of fulfillment.

"By declaring that man is responsible and must actualize the potential meaning of his life, I wish to stress that the true meaning of life is to be discovered in the world rather than within man or his own psyche, as though it were a closed system. I have termed this constitutive characteristic "the self-transcendence of human existence." It denotes the fact that being human always points, and is directed, to something or someone, other than oneself—be it a meaning to fulfill or another human being to encounter. The more one forgets himself—by giving himself to a cause to serve or another person to love—the more human he is and the more he actualizes himself. What is called self-actualization is not an attainable aim at all, for the simple reason that the more one would strive for it, the more he would miss it. In other words, self-actualization is possible only as a side-effect of self-transcendence."—Viktor E. Frankl, Man's Search for Meaning

Viktor Frankl is telling us that we find transcendence or Transformational Leadership through loving others and serving them. When a person lays himself aside and serves others without expecting anything in return, it is transformational. It changes eternity.

Transformational leadership happens when we demonstrate commitment to and provide clarity of the THERE to create synergy and unity with the team. We have to share the current reality of the HERE with transparency based on facts and not on feelings or assumptions. Finally, we have to intervene when there is a lack of clarity or current reality for the HERE to help the team have a shared mental model of how to negotiate the PATH. When we do these things, we are creating an environment people will want to be a part of.

Matthew 6: 1-4

Take heed that you do not do your charitable deeds before men, to be seen by them. Otherwise you have no reward from your Father in heaven. Therefore, when you do a charitable deed, do not sound a trumpet before you as the hypocrites do in the synagogues and in the streets, that they may have glory from men. Assuredly, I say to you, they have their reward. But when you do a charitable deed, do not let your left hand know what your right hand is doing, that your charitable deed may be in secret; and your Father who sees in secret will Himself reward you openly. NKJV

Jesus is explaining that when we are doing for others, we really need to be introspective of our motives. If we are serving others, it shouldn't be towards receiving anything in return to include praise for our deeds. When we do good deeds and then tell everyone how good we are, we are being transactional. We are actually doing those deeds so that everyone will know what we did and think better of us. When we do good deeds expecting nothing in return because it is just a part of who we are, it is transformational.

Questioning why we do things helps us know our HERE. Did I do this for others (serving the WE THERE) or did I do it for myself in some way (serving the ME THERE)? When working on our values or pillars to gain influence, it should be to serve others and not ourselves. We should want to have a greater influence with others to show how to do life the way God intended us to live it. This influence, through referent power helps us use transformational leadership to create a culture of giving and serving others.

CHAPTER 4

Freedom VS Control

(HERE Tool #2)

"The one thing you can't take away from me is the way I choose to respond to what you do to me. The last of one's freedoms is to choose one's attitude in any given circumstance."—Viktor E. Frankl

Now that we have a clear transcendent THERE and we have some idea of our current reality in relation to power and leadership styles, we can dive deeper into our HERE with the second HERE tool. The second HERE tool is Freedom vs Control.

FREEDOM

When our THERE is clear and we are committed to it, it can be tempting to try to control others to come with you. This can be done through numerous forms of manipulation. However, to truly allow others to become transformational means that they have to choose to do what is right, because it is right. We should invite others to join us on the journey in life but we cannot control them. They are free to make their own choices.

Instead of controlling others, we want to hope, pray and encourage others down the road of life and when necessary exhort and rebuke. This will help provide a structure for them to work towards what we call self-governance. This structure is called the Freedom V.

The Freedom V can be looked at from two different perspectives. It can be viewed from a perspective of how to lead oneself and how to lead others.

The key points of the freedom V is that structure demands behavior. We must have clear expectations and consequences to promote self-governance. The larger V is created using clear expectations and clear consequences.

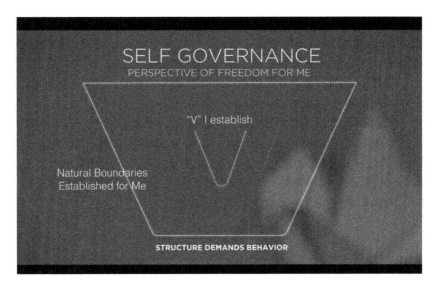

In the picture above, we can see the boundaries created for us in the larger V. This depicts a structure put in place through a law of nature, your employer or anyone in a position of authority (expectations and consequences). The smaller V in the middle is a structure we create because we are self-governed. For instance, if your supervisor tells you that you have to be to work by 0800 (the boundary of the bigger V), you may put a structure in place for yourself that gets you to work by 0750 every day. You have created a structure that creates accountability for yourself (the smaller V). You have limited your own freedom so others do not have to. Self-governance means that you do what is right because it is right and not out of fear of consequence or reprisal. It is limiting your own freedom so others don't have to. It is more palatable to us to limit our own freedom that have others do it.

There are areas of our life that we are more self-governed in than others. We can see this with our pillars and values. If you are very good with your finances, you probably have a lot of structure in place for yourself. You may do a monthly budget, write out clear financial goals or have an accountability partner who checks in with you on how you are doing with your money. All of this may sound very restrictive and that's the point. You have established a structure (small V) within the larger structure. The larger structure would be formed by a boundary such as not paying your bills will result in legal action, repossession of material possessions, or possibly jail time.

With another pillar, you may not be as self-governed. Let's use the physical pillar as an example. The larger V boundaries are established by laws such as a certain weight, blood pressure or cholesterol number may result in death. If you continue to cross those boundaries, there will probably be consequences that could even include your death. You are free to do this but it is probably not in your best interest.

I Corinthians 6: 12

All things are lawful for me, but all things are not helpful. All things are lawful for me, but I will not be brought under the power of any.-NKJV

I Corinthians 10: 23

All things are lawful for me, but not all things are helpful; all things are lawful for me, but not all things edify. Let no one seek his own, but each one the other's well-being.-NKJV

Paul is telling us that just because some things are legal for us to do doesn't mean it is beneficial for us to do them. Just because the law allows, it doesn't make it helpful for us. The Freedom V we create for ourselves inside of what the law gives us, prevents us from doing these things that are not good for us. That structure we create keeps us from being brought under the influence of those unhelpful things.

As leaders at work, in social organizations or in our families, we provide structure for our subordinates or children to help them choose the right actions. To create a structure to help others make good choices, we have to provide them clear expectations and consequences to help them stay within the Freedom V. We create these boundaries using our five types of power. We use our position and coercive power to create the outer boundaries and then referent, reward and expert to influence them to stay in the V.

You will notice clear expectations and consequences are key to this. Clarity of these two items are what make all the difference in using this tool. If the boundary created is not clear or even a little fuzzy, it is very difficult for others to stay within the structure. We use our position power to lay out the structure and the coercive power to lay out the consequences should our subordinate decide to cross that boundary. Hopefully we, instead, will be able to utilize reward, expert and referent power to keep them within the structure. Our personal example of staying inside the structure is critical for this.

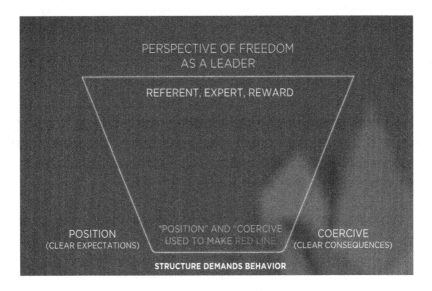

If my THERE for raising my children is along the lines of "raising good adults capable of making good decisions", this tool is especially useful. When a child is younger, we have them very tight in the Freedom V. Children come into this world separated from God. As parents, we look at them as beautiful little angels. In reality, they are quite the opposite. They have to be taught how to share, taught how to love, taught how to be responsible and taught how to not make life about ME. To do this we have to start children off in the bottom of the Freedom V with a lot of structure. They are told what time to wake up, what time to go to bed, to eat and even play. They learn that they are on a schedule and that if they choose to violate the clear rules provided for them there will be consequences. As the child grows older and demonstrate more maturity, they are given a wider V to make their own choices with a little more freedom. They may get a later bed time or time to be home. If they violate that time, they have crossed the boundary and suffer the consequences. As the child gets even older they receive more freedom. They may get the car keys and told to be home by 10:00 PM. If they continue to show good faith, they may be given more freedom and if they step across that boundary, they may find themselves pulled down in the freedom V a bit. We see this done for us in scripture over and over again.

Genesis 2: 16-17

And the LORD **God commanded the man, saying, "Of every tree of the garden you may freely eat; but of the tree of the knowledge of good and evil you shall not eat, for in the day that you eat of it you shall surely die."-NKJV**

With Adam, God gave some very clear expectations for how to conduct himself. He told Adam that he could eat from any tree in the garden but not from the Tree of Knowledge of Good and Evil. God also lays out the consequences should Adam decide to cross the boundary of the Freedom V. He was told the consequence of violating the structure God provided was death.

God gives us a great example of how to do this for others in our lives. He communicates the expectations and consequences very clearly. He grants Adam the ability to make his own choices for his actions and lets him know what will happen should he choose to make poor decisions. God didn't try to control Adam. He let him choose his own fate. This is exactly what we should be doing with our children and those we are responsible for.

When raising children, we often see this principle turned upside down, literally. Children are given an upside down V. When they are little, they are given too much freedom and are allowed to do whatever they like. As they get older, the parents start to realize their child is on a terrible trajectory and will not be self-governed or capable of making good decisions on their own. This causes the parents to try to clamp down on them with an attempt to control them. The issue is exacerbated as the child begins to rebel and it makes matters even worse. Using the Freedom V properly and following through with coercive and reward power can create the understanding of transactional leadership which can later be grown towards transformational.

This principle works well with new employees as well. We want to put people out in the Freedom V as far as we can without going too far. If we don't provide enough structure for people, they will flounder and fail. We want to give them all the freedom they can handle but not more. When people demonstrate that they are self-governed, they don't need a bunch of rules to get them to do what they should be doing. They will create their own structure to keep them in their own Freedom V.

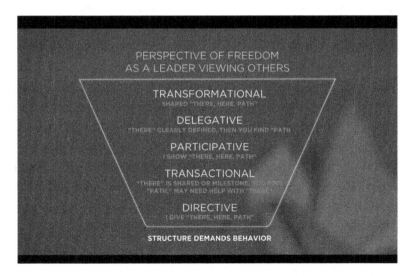

The leadership styles, shown above, are another way to help us understand how to use the Freedom V. We can see that we should be using the directive leadership when someone is down low in the Freedom V. As they move out further, we want to use other leadership styles to allow them more freedom. When we finally reach transformational leadership, we have a shared There-Here-Path and people are more likely to be self-governed. This simply means they will restrict their own freedom so someone else won't have to.

Leaders who can apply this principle understand how complex it can be. Adults typically reside in multiple planes along the inside of the Freedom V at one time. You may have someone who is very self-governed in one area of their life but needs more structure in another. Pulling the person all the way back down in the Freedom V can be catastrophic. You may need to provide more clarity of expectations and consequences for one aspect of their job or life but not in others. For instance if your child isn't cleaning his room properly but all other chores are being done without asking, you wouldn't want to put structures in place for the other chores being done correctly. That will just cause them to rebel. Provide the structure to help them clean their room and allow them to continue to demonstrate good judgement where they have proven to do so already. The same is true in the workplace. If someone is transformational in some areas but not others, address the areas in which they need help with more structure solely.

A good litmus test for having the right structures, clarity of expectations or clarity of consequences in place could be to count how many orders you give every day. If you find yourself giving orders all the time, you are probably missing a structure, clarity or rule that can help prevent this. Having others make the correct decision on their own can alleviate a lot of time and effort on the part of the parent or manager. In the military we call this decentralized command.

CONTROL

Providing structure for others does not mean controlling them. They still have a choice. Did Adam and Eve have a choice? They chose to eat the fruit and had to suffer the consequences. We cannot control others. In fact, there are only three things in life we can control. We can control whom we trust, our attitude/perspective, and our actions.

One of the great paradoxes of life is that if we want more influence with others, we have to give up control. This sounds counterintuitive to most people. When you try to control others, they will rebel. When you try to force them to do something, they will resist. However, when you make it their idea, let them have the appropriate amount of autonomy, and make them responsible for it, they will be much more invested. This will open doors for us to influence them. When we try to control them or their actions, they will resist and not want to come to us for advice. Instead, they will come to us to make decisions for them. Dependency is good for our ego, but not for the growth of those we are serving. This will limit their personal growth and require us to continue to make all of the decisions. When we don't try to control others, they will be more likely to come to us for advice and help. To have more influence you have to give up control.

The reality is we cannot control others. There are over seven billion people in the world and we get to control one of them. No matter how hard we try through any technique we use, we cannot control others. They are free to make any decision they wish. We cannot even control our children. That statement usually rubs someone the wrong way but it is true. Our children are free to make their own choices. Those choices may come with severe consequences but they can still choose to do what the structure we have provided them says to do or they can choose to step across the boundary.

"The one thing you can't take away from me is the way I choose to respond to what you do to me. The last of one's freedoms is to choose one's attitude in any given circumstance."—Viktor E. Frankl

Viktor Frankl was in a concentration camp. He still had choices. He could still choose his attitude. He could still choose who he trusted. He could still control his actions. We may think we control our children but no one can be controlled. We can put a very strict structure around others that have very strict consequences, but they still have choices, internally and externally. Very few situations we could possibly put others in come close to the structures the concentration camps provided Viktor Frankl. However, he recognized that he still had choices.

This leads us to another great dichotomy of control. When you attempt to control other peoples' choices, they end up controlling you. As you try to get them to do what you think is in their best interest (control them), you are attempting to take away freedom. This is not possible. When they feel you are taking freedom away from them, they will probably rebel. Their actions, or lack thereof, causes you to be upset or react. They are now controlling you. You can give people the best advice possible to do what's in their best interest but it is still their choice. Not everyone will make the journey. We can only invite them along. They must choose to take a step down the path.

Have you ever tried to control your spouse? What are the results of this? When they don't do what you want, your emotions start to show. Their actions or lack thereof are now controlling you. If you don't like others controlling you, the answer is very simple. Don't try to control others or that is exactly what will happen.

THREE THINGS WE CAN CONTROL

1. WHOM WE TRUST:

2. OUR ATTITUDE/PERSPECTIVE:

3. OUR ACTIONS:

The first thing we can control is whom we trust. Ultimately this is the fundamental decision of life. Do you trust God or do you trust someone other than God? When we recognize God is in control and not us, it is freeing. We can expand this to trusting others to share truth with us. Do you have someone in your life that you can trust to share truth with you? Being someone who can be counted on to share truth with others will help them find their HERE. Having someone you can trust to share truth with you, will help you find your HERE.

The second item we get to control is our attitude or perspective. We can control how we view things. This is heavily influenced by the first item we get to control. Do I believe God is in control and that he has me right where I am for a reason? If I believe God has me where he wants me, I can look at circumstances in my life differently. I can choose to understand that God has me where I am for a reason and instead of having a poor attitude I can choose to ask what I should be learning right now. Our attitude or perspective is often a reflection of our THERE. I can choose to affect life, people and circumstances or I can choose to let them affect me.

A good friend of mine, Dianne Pass, lost her husband John a few years ago. He had a protracted illness that had him bedridden and in constant discomfort. In her book *Lessons in Living and dying*, she tells how, one day towards the end, John got a bit cranky and got a little short with her. He very quickly realized what he was doing and immediately apologized. He stated that maybe he couldn't do anything for himself anymore but he could choose to have a better attitude for Dianne. He could choose his perspective of serving her by not being cranky.

"We who lived in concentration camps can remember the men who walked through the huts comforting others, giving away their last piece of bread. They may have been few in number, but they offer sufficient proof that everything can be taken from a man but one thing: the last of the human freedoms—to choose one's attitude in any given set of circumstances, to choose one's own way."—Viktor E. Frankl

The third item we can control is our actions. We can choose to change item number one (whom we trust), we can choose to take a time out and reset our emotions, we can reassess our HERE, we can change our THERE, or we can take a step down the path. However, we cannot choose to control other peoples' choices. We can provide influence. We can provide advice. We can provide structure. But we cannot control their actions.

Matthew 7: 1-6

"Judge not, that you be not judged. For with what judgment you judge, you will be judged; and with the measure you use, it will be measured back to you. And why do you look at the speck in your brother's eye, but do not consider the plank in your own eye? Or how can you say to your brother, 'Let me remove the speck from your eye'; and look, a plank *is* in your own eye? Hypocrite! First remove the plank from your own eye, and then you will see clearly to remove the speck from your brother's eye. "Do not give what is holy to the dogs; nor cast your pearls before swine,

lest they trample them under their feet, and turn and tear you in pieces.-NKJV

In the scripture reading above, Jesus is helping us see that we often observe what needs to be "fixed" in others very easily. However, the problem is that we see these usually minor issues in others and miss our own current reality. We see the speck in their eye but look past the plank in our own. When we see the wrong in others, it is usually because we have the same wrong in us on a bigger scale. Instead of focusing on controlling others, focus on controlling the three things we can control. If you want to affect change, start with changing yourself. Start by being a good example of what right looks like.

When we look back to the story of LTC Joshua Chamberlain and the 20th Maine defending Little Round Top, we can see this tool play out very clearly. When the 20th Maine encountered the 13 Sharpshooters who were deserting, he could have had them shot. Instead, he chose a different course. He gave them a choice. He told them they could go back to Maine or they could go with the 20th Maine to Little Round Top. Chamberlain went a step further. He gave them very clear expectations. He told them that if they went into battle with his unit, they would be expected to fight. He invited them to be a part of the 20th Maine. What would have happened had Chamberlain forced the men to go along with his unit? They probably would have run at the first sounds of gunfire while the 20th Maine's attention was occupied elsewhere. Instead, they were invited along. They were a part of the unit and they fought. Those 13 men provided the lethal fire that by all accounts was decisive to the Confederate attack being repelled. Without them there and fighting, history may have turned out differently.

Chamberlain understood this simple truth. He understood that you cannot control others. Because of his understanding and application of this principle, he was able to complete his mission and change history.

When we understand God is in control it affects our attitude or perspective, especially when things in our life seem to be difficult. When we have the attitude that God has us where he wants us for a reason, it affects the actions we take. When you see yourself making poor choices, it is usually a result of a poor perspective. When you have a poor perspective, it is usually a result of not trusting God.

The Freedom V is a great tool to move our children from selfish creatures to good adults capable of making good decisions on their own. It is good to help us understand how to set structures in place to keep us from crossing a boundary that will result in consequences. It is a good tool to help us show others that we are moving them in the V to give them more structure to serve them or giving them less structure because they have demonstrated self-governance in that aspect of their job or life.

The three things we can control helps us understand that we cannot control others. We can only control ourselves. If we try to control others, they end up controlling us. If we want more influence we have to give up control.

Understanding where we are in the Freedom V with respect to ourselves, helps us understand our HERE a little better. Knowing how self-governed we are in different areas of our lives helps us know where we may need more structure from ourselves or with the help of others.

CHAPTER 5

The Project Mood Curve

(HERE Tool #3)

The Project Mood Curve is the PATH that links the HERE to the THERE. Everything in life follows this pattern. The only difference between PATHs will be the depth of the "pit of despair."

The third HERE tool is the Project Mood Curve. The Project Mood Curve is the PATH that life takes. It is the link between HERE and THERE. So, the logical question is why not call it a PATH tool? As we move down the PATH by exerting energy and commitment to take a step towards our THERE, our HERE just changed. We are now at our new HERE and have to reassess it to know where we are. The PATH is a series of Milestones and new HEREs.

MOOD CURVE

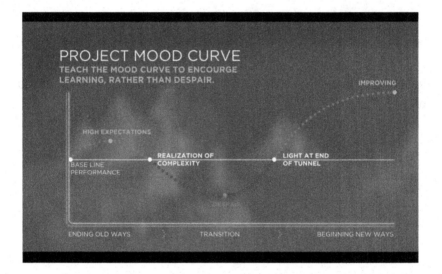

The graph above depicts the PATH that life and all projects follow. It is true with all things. The only difference is the depth of the "pit of despair". The X Axis is time while the Y Axis is level of excitement. Starting on the left side, we go into a project or phase of life with very high expectations and motivation. As time goes by, we begin to transition from the way we were doing things to the new way. The level of motivation or excitement starts to go down as we realize the project or phase is going to be more difficult than previously anticipated. The pit of despair can be difficult to get out of and it is generally where most people give up. However, if we stay committed to the THERE, we start to see the end in sight and begin improving as we start doing things the new way habitually.

Let's look at this in terms of something simple. Let's look at your exercise program. When New Year's Day rolls around you are getting ready to start your new diet and exercise program with an awesome Milestone goal to lose 10 pounds. You have a high degree of excitement and anticipation so you are on the blue dot of High Expectations in the graph. After your first day, you start to realize how much work this is really going to be. You are sore and you are hungry because rice cakes taste terrible and you are going through carbohydrate and sugar withdrawal. You have just entered the "Pit of Despair." The only difference between your Mood Curve and someone else's is the depth of this pit. For some, this will be easier than others. This is where most people lose sight of the THERE for their goal. They tend to not be able to see how this is going to be possible. However, with commitment to the THERE and willpower your body and mind begin to adjust. Your taste buds get used to not having the sugars and the cravings dissipate. You quit getting as sore from the workouts as your muscles become stronger and now you start to see results. You begin to see the light at the end of the tunnel. The commitment to the THERE becomes easier because you have now formed a habit, which takes less energy to work at something than when starting something. An object in motion tends to stay in motion (kinetic energy) while an object at rest tends to stay at rest (potential energy). You start to see positive results and begin improving. You are on a roll and the diet and exercise take less willpower. You have made it through the pit of despair and now the mood curve trajectory has flattened out.

You can see this in every facet of your life from taking a college class where you are excited to start or beginning a new job. In your college class, several things can go wrong right off the bat. Your professor may have had the older version of the textbook on the syllabus and all of the test questions come from a version you don't have and there are a lot of external issues in life that seem to come to a head all at once. You move into the pit very quickly. However, sticking with it and being committed allows us to move through the pit. Everyone in the class is going through the same thing. The only difference is that some of the other students will not have a pit as deep as yours and some will be deeper.

It can just be helpful to know that you are not struggling alone and that whenever you start something new you should not expect it to go as planned. Armed with the knowledge that you will hit a pit of despair can actually lessen the depth of the pit. You know that your current reality (HERE) at the beginning will be excited and underestimate the struggles involved. When you start moving down the PATH, you soon recognize that you are in the pit of despair. Understanding that this is a normal part of everything helps you to stay committed and you soon start improving.

BUILDING HABITS

Research shows that it normally takes 17-21 repetitions of something to build a habit. When you hit week three of your diet and exercise program, you are generally moving out of the pit of despair because the task has become habitual. It now takes less will power. Research also shows that willpower is an exhaustible resource. The experts will even tell you that if you have a moral decision to make, make it in the morning. They say this because by the end of the day you have less willpower available. Your tank is empty. There are some very famous experiments that demonstrate this with the Marshmallow Experiment as well as the Radish and Chocolate Chip Cookie Experiment, both of which you can watch on the internet. The bottom line is that people who are forced to use willpower to resist something will have less willpower to resist other things later. You see this very often with smokers who quit smoking and then gain weight. They are using all of their willpower to not smoke and don't have the energy or willpower available to stick to their diet as well.

Research has also shown that Christians tend to have more willpower than Non-Christians. Christians tend to have healthier teeth, manage their money better, live longer and overall be healthier. Why is this? How would a religious affiliation cause me to have more willpower? The answer is simple. Christians have the ability to tap into an inexhaustible resource. They can tap into the Holy Spirit. They don't have to rely on themselves to see them through their struggles. It comes down to the first item we get to control; whom you trust. Do I trust God or someone other than God? Our faith gives us access to this resource to help us through these tough times, this pit of despair.

Isaiah 40: 29-31

He gives power to the weak and to *those who have* no might He increases strength. Even the youths shall faint and be weary, and the young men shall utterly fall, but those who wait on the Lᴏʀᴅ shall renew *their* strength; they shall mount up with wings like eagles, they shall run and not be weary, they shall walk and not faint.-NKJV

Philippians 4: 13

I can do all things through Christ who strengthens me.-NKJV

ACTS 1: 4-8

And being assembled together with *them*, He commanded them not to depart from Jerusalem, but to wait for the Promise of the Father, "which," *He said,* "you have heard from Me; for John truly baptized with water, but you shall

be baptized with the Holy Spirit not many days from now." Therefore, when they had come together, they asked Him, saying, "Lord, will You at this time restore the kingdom to Israel?" And He said to them, "It is not for you to know times or seasons which the Father has put in His own authority. But you shall receive power when the Holy Spirit has come upon you; and you shall be witnesses to Me in Jerusalem, and in all Judea and Samaria, and to the end of the earth.-NKJV

As the scripture verses shows, we can do all things through God. Jesus dwells within us in the form of the Holy Spirit. We can tap into that inexhaustible energy source any time we choose to. Listening to what God would have us do helps us build our THERE. It will take commitment and energy along that PATH. Trusting that God is in control and using the energy of the Holy Spirit allows us to accomplish anything.

TEAM BUILDING

Let's take a look at the Project Mood Curve from the perspective of team building. The team building stages are Forming, Storming, Norming, Performing and sometimes Adjourning. The forming stage is where the team first comes together. There is generally a great deal of excitement to start out on a new PATH together. Soon after forming people start to vie for position. They try to figure out where they fit into the team and what role they will fulfill. This is called the Storming phase. Once everyone has a role and figure out what their part is to be, they begin to progress and start the Norming phase. This is where the group's unwritten rules become the norms for operating together. Finally the team begins to really make progress towards the THERE and they are performing. The final step is the Adjourning phase. This is where the team has an opportunity to look back and do an after action review to determine lessons learned that they can apply to their next project together or for other teams.

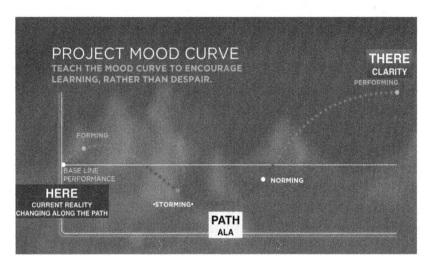

In the graph above, you can see the forming stage is where we are excited about the new team or project. As the project gets underway and the team comes together, our HERE has moved along the PATH and into the storming phase. This is the pit of despair. People are vying for control and trying to figure out where they fit into it all. The pit of despair is where we need to do a lot of ALA (act-learn-adjust) to be successful. If we stay committed to the THERE, we continue to take steps down the PATH where our HERE continues to change and we start norming. Norms are unwritten rules that everyone adopts. The team begins to see productivity and things seem to move more quickly. As the team continues down the PATH, the HERE (current reality) changes to the performing phase of team development. The team is very effective at this point and work together well.

Looking back at our story of Chamberlain and the 20th Maine on Little Round Top. Where did they hit the pit of despair? They bottomed out in the pit after the second charge up the hill by the Confederates. The 20th Maine was down to two bullets per man and one third of the force was dead or wounded. They were deep in the pit. However, this is where real leadership happens. When things aren't going well, leaders need to lead. When the team can't see the light at the end of the tunnel and things look hopeless, leaders step up and clarify the THERE. They focus the team. They lead by example. We saw Chamberlain do exactly that. He drew his sabre, and though wounded himself, led the charge down the hill. When things go wrong in your team, do you lead? When things go wrong in your family, do you lead? The pit of despair is where real leadership is most evident. It is where leaders give hope to others through their personal example of doing life right and helping others see the THERE of doing life the way God intended it.

Mood Curve for Marriage

As an example of team building and how it falls into the Project Mood Curve, let's use marriage. We hope that prior to the marriage, the happy couple has established a THERE for their marriage. We will say that this couple has established ONENESS as their THERE. They have clarity of what that means. They know that oneness means he must provide security for her and she must provide significance for him and they both must bring God into the equation above all else for this to work. As the wedding day approaches, the excitement for they happy couple begins to build. This is especially true for the bride who has probably built this day up and dreamed about it since she was a small child. The ceremony is pulled off with only a few minor glitches, which no one remembers five minutes later. The happy couple goes on their honeymoon and all is right with life.

Soon after the honeymoon the new team departs from the Forming stage and enters the Storming stage. They realize the THERE became the ceremony and not the marriage. They accomplished the ceremony and there can be a little bit of a depression that sets in with accomplishing your THERE whether you intended it to be your THERE or not. They let the milestone of the ceremony eclipse the Transcendent THERE of ONENESS. There may be a little bit of the "now what?" going on. They start making their marriage about ME instead of WE. They are both trying to figure out their roles. They came from different backgrounds where he opened presents on Christmas Eve and she opened on Christmas Day. The struggles continue because it turns out that he likes Crest Toothpaste and she likes Colgate. He squeezes the tube from the bottom while she blasphemously squeezes from the middle.

As they learn to work through conflict resolution and build their own traditions for the next 3-5 years, they begin the Norming phase of the marriage. They have their own family norms now and start to really make progress towards ONENESS. Next, they enter the performing phase; they have committed to try to pursue the other's best, patiently, kindly, sacrificially and unconditionally. They have become closer to God through all of this and are working towards that Transcendent THERE of ONENESS.

Genesis 2: 24

Therefore a man shall leave his father and mother and be joined to his wife, and they shall become one flesh.-NKJV

Ephesians 5: 22-33

Wives, submit to your own husbands, as to the Lord. For the husband is head of the wife, as also Christ is head of the church; and He is the Savior of the body. Therefore, just as the church is subject to Christ, so *let* the wives *be* to their own husbands in everything.

Husbands, love your wives, just as Christ also loved the church and gave Himself for her, that He might sanctify and

cleanse her with the washing of water by the word, that He might present her to Himself a glorious church, not having spot or wrinkle or any such thing, but that she should be holy and without blemish. So husbands ought to love their own wives as their own bodies; he who loves his wife loves himself. For no one ever hated his own flesh, but nourishes and cherishes it, just as the Lord *does* the church. For we are members of His body of His flesh and of His bones. "For this reason a man shall leave his father and mother and be joined to his wife, and the two shall become one flesh." This is a great mystery, but I speak concerning Christ and the church. Nevertheless let each one of you in particular so love his own wife as himself, and let the wife *see* that she respects *her* husband.-NKJV

The scripture readings above help us understand the THERE for marriage. God shows us that Oneness is what he intends for a marriage. In Ephesians, Paul goes on to explain what this looks like. When a woman respects her husband and provides him significance she is giving him what he needs. When a man loves his wife as himself and provides her with security, he is giving her what she needs. This means that no matter what happens she is his biggest fan and he provides her not with just physical security but with emotional, spiritual and mental security as well. Men need to feel like they are significant and women need to feel like they are secure in all areas of their lives. When we do this for each other and bring God into the equation, we have Oneness.

What keeps us from finding Oneness? What keeps her from providing him with significance? What keeps him from providing her the security she needs? What keeps both him and her from focusing on God? We have the We THERE of Oneness so what can keep us from reaching it? It's the Me THERE. Me gets in the way. I know that what's best for me is doing what's best for her and she knows what's in her best interest is doing what's best for him. Yet we consistently serve ourselves instead of our spouse. To prevent this from happening, we have to focus on the THERE.

Mood Curve for Children

Our story for the happy couple continues when they are about to have their first child. They communicate well and establish the THERE for child rearing: to GROW A GOOD ADULT CAPABLE OF MAKING GOOD DECISIONS ON THEIR OWN. The excitement builds with the baby showers and the attention from friends and family. The young couple is in the forming phase.

Once the baby is born they immediately enter into the storming phase. We have added a new, temporary member of the team. This particular team member does not sleep at night, eats all the time, gets sick every week and fills the diaper way too often. After a couple of years, the child begins to be a little more self-sufficient and we start norming, but then we enter the "terrible twos" where the parents regret ever wondering when the child would ever walk because it gets into everything. We slide back down into the pit. Proper use of the Freedom V gets us through this stage and the family begins norming once again. Many years later, the child is now a teenager who wants more freedom than the parents are ready to give. We enter a new mood curve again. Once again, the parents apply the proper use of the Freedom V and the child turns 18 and is armed with the capability to Make Good Decisions on his or her own and leaves the team. The team has entered the Adjourning phase.

In child rearing, we use the Freedom V to help grow our children into capable adults. Helping them see that they are not the most important team member is also very important. They need to see what a marriage, done right, looks like. Their relationships will often take the same course as the ones role modeled for them. Demonstrating that your spouse is the most important person in your life and that ONENESS is the THERE for marriage will help the child prioritize their spouse in the relationships they will have in the future. The child is a very important, *temporary* member of the team but not the most important member of the team. You and your spouse are the permanent team members and the leaders of the team, not the child. Seeing this relationship play out and helping them see what a successful marriage and healthy relationship is all about is the most effective way to help them become good adults capable of making good decisions on their own.

I am not advocating for child neglect but I am advocating for modeling what Oneness should be. When we lead by example and demonstrate what a marriage should be instead of what society and culture in our country tells us, we are setting up our children's' chances of success. This also prevents the "empty nest syndrome" from happening.

When we understand that every project, relationship or any endeavor we undertake will go through the process of the Project Mood Curve, we can mentally prepare ourselves for the challenges we will face. Having the proper perspective of expectations assists us in remaining committed to the THERE. We know that it is just part of the journey. The only difference between one person's mood curve and another's is the depth of the pit. Some people will have an easier PATH than others due to having a better understanding of their HERE, being able to Act/Learn/Adjust quicker on entering the mood curve or they may have more clarity of their THERE.

Leadership or lack of leadership becomes much more magnified when we are in the Pit of Despair. The "pit" is where leadership really happens. It is easy to be the leader of the group during the forming stage and during the performing stage of team building. Most anyone can lead during the times when people are excited to be there or operating effectively as a team. However, when things are difficult, there is conflict amongst the team, or we lose sight of the THERE, real leadership makes itself known. Do you lead? Do you lead your family when things aren't going well? Do you lead at your work when things are tough? When we look at your earlier list of the greatest heroes, there is usually a common thread. They stayed committed to the THERE through the worst possible times. They overcame huge obstacles or unsurmountable odds to get THERE. Their Pit of Despair was very deep but they led others through it. That's what made them great.

CHAPTER 6

Seek and Share Truth

(HERE Tool #4)

*Adopted from Managerial Moment of Truth by Robert Fritz

Sharing truth serves the WE THERE. Choosing not to share truth serves the ME THERE.

Up to this point in the book, we have mentioned clarity of expectations and consequences many times. As you will recall, the Freedom V is created with clear expectations and clear consequences. We have also stated several times that we struggle to know our current reality. The way we help others understand that their actions are not meeting expectations, they don't have a clear understanding of their current reality (HERE) or they don't have clarity of the THERE is by Sharing Truth.

This tool is used to help people clarify their HERE. We generally don't have an accurate understanding of our HERE. We typically think we are better at things or doing a better job at things than we really are. When we don't have clarity of our current reality we can have a moment of truth with ourselves or hopefully we have someone in our lives that we trust who will have a moment of truth with us.

The point of the MOT is to help people see that they need to change one or more of the three things they can control. They either need to change whom they trust, their attitude or their actions. We want them to do this so that they can continue to be a member of the team.

Sharing truth is generally one of the more difficult things we will do in our lives. Sharing truth could create conflict but we should value people enough to develop them anyways. We should value people enough to provide clear expectations and clear consequences. Finally we should have the moral courage to share truth when actual doesn't meet expected.

A Moment of Truth does not have to be uncomfortable or full of conflict if we have a culture of sharing truth. Having such a culture is rare in most places, teams or families. When we measure small and measure often, we are continuously sharing truth with grace and mercy. It can become ingrained in the culture of our family, team or organization to the point that it is just how you do business. However, when we don't measure small and often, the emotions can build and a Moment of Truth can turn into conflict instead of serving others. To avoid the conflict-filled emotional blow outs we have to first make sure that we are talking about truth and not feelings or opinion.

Opinion is the same as speculating and assuming. When we don't have the facts, we fill in the blanks with our own opinions. If you start a Moment of Truth with the "I feel like" you aren't doing a good job, you are not dealing with facts. We need to look at SMART expectations of others that did not get met.

People tend to not conduct a MOT because they are more worried about managing the emotions of others instead of managing truth. They may also not conduct a MOT because they are more worried about damaging the relationship with the team member rather than sharing truth with them. Both of these factors are self-focused and not others focused. If we have a good Transcendent THERE that focuses on serving others instead of ourselves we will look past these two items and have the courage to share truth despite them.

We often see the MOT process happen in the pit of despair, or storming phase, of the mood curve. This is where people haven't figured out how to work well together yet. They may not completely understand the goals or THERE for the team and will need help with understanding their current reality (HERE). The pit of despair is also where we tend to see more violations of the Freedom V structure or people trying to control others. All of these require leaders to lead. Leaders lead through sharing truth with others. They demonstrate they care enough about their team members to lay themselves aside and help others see truth.

MOMENT OF TRUTH

TRUTH NOT OPINION

- Without Truth, people and organizations flounder and fail.

- Opinion is the same as speculation and assumption.

- We often fill in the blanks with opinion rather than searching for facts.

- Opinion often prevails over truth, when opinion is held by one in power.

Knowing that most of us have a current reality (HERE) of not sharing truth well, we can expect a Moment of Truth to create conflict. However, we should value people enough to develop them anyways. We should be more afraid of stagnancy in life than conflict. We need to act when actual does not meet expected. Many of us will struggle with that simple sentence and we won't act. This is normally a reflection of the ME THERE instead of the WE THERE. The ME THERE doesn't want to have to deal with conflict or feeling uncomfortable. The WE THERE is about valuing others and serving them. If we value others, we should share truth with them.

Have you ever known someone who was let go from their job and really never even had any warning that their performance was not meeting expectations? They were given a laundry list of things that they have been doing wrong for the past weeks or months and no one cared enough about them to demonstrate the courage to even tell them. How can we expect people to change their behavior or actions without helping them see that what they are doing is not acceptable? When asked if you would want others to share truth with you, the answer is almost always a resounding yes. Why then, do we struggle to share truth with others? In serving others, we should pursue their best unconditionally.

We now know that most of us have a difficult time knowing what our HERE is. We struggle to know our own current reality. Helping others see their current reality by doing the MOT correctly can be rewarding and fulfilling. It can also be full of conflict and emotion when not done correctly.

A Moment of Truth is a four step process. The four steps are acknowledge reality, get the story, create a plan and give feedback. This can be done formally or informally. This process doesn't need to be awkward. It can be part of a normal conversation and should happen all of the time. Most times that a MOT is conducted, the recipient of the MOT won't even realize what just happened. They will just know that they have gained clarity of their HERE and now have a better plan to get THERE.

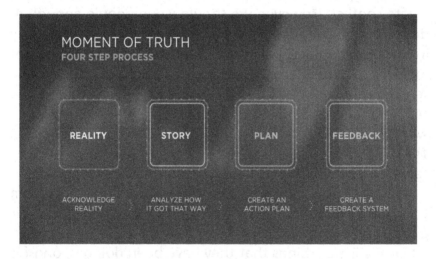

MOT Step 1

The first step of a Moment of Truth (MOT) starts with simply acknowledging reality. This may sound easy but it is usually by far the most difficult of the four steps. To assist us with this we use digital or binary thinking. Binary thinking is using opposites to ask questions-simply asking yes or no, true or false, up or down, etc.

Let's say one of the people at your work who reports to you has been showing up late all week. We can start the conversation by saying, "Can we agree that you are supposed to be here at 0800 every day and you have been showing up later than 0900 all week?" We have left them with two answers. They can answer yes or no. This doesn't leave room for them to start getting into the story. We just want them to state the reality of the situation. It is normal for them to throw a curveball at this point and start with the "yes buts". Yes I was late but my car broke down one day, I had a flat tire the next and my alarm quit working. At this point, we are not trying to get the story so we go back to step one by saying, "I appreciate all of that and I do want to talk about how it got this way but can we agree that you were supposed to be here at 0800 every day and you have been showing up later than 0900, yes or no?" Each time they start trying to skip to step two, we need to bring them back to step one and help them acknowledge that their actual performance did not meet the expectations.

The example of being late is pretty simplistic. Many times a Moment of Truth (MOT) will be about a much more complex expectation that has not been met. However, they all work the same. We either met expectations or we didn't. When we set clear expectations for our children, each other and our direct reports at work, it helps us be able to serve others through MOT. The MOT happens when someone violates the boundaries of the Freedom V or when their opinion of themselves isn't close to current reality.

MOT Step 2

Step two is get the story. There are usually a lot of reasons why someone does not meet expectations but usually people don't willfully and deliberately try to underperform. We all want to be great. Sometimes we find that missing the expectation is just a symptom of a much deeper and underlying problem in someone's life. We have to be prepared for that when doing a MOT. They may have had a recent death in the family, be going through a divorce or have medical issues. The facts remain that actual did not meet expected but now when we go into step three, we can address the root cause of the problem and not the symptom.

Sometimes the moment of truth ends up being nothing more than a clarification of the expectations. When we get the story, we may find out that we didn't make the expectations clear enough. This is a leader issue with communication and an opportunity to create clarity.

It will be important to use more open-ended questions in step two. This will lead to self-discovery, learning and more mentoring than teaching. Open ended questions are good but it is usually best to avoid "why" questions. "Why" questions can make us feel like we are being implicated and cause defensiveness. It is usually better to ask "tell me more about" questions, "how" questions or "what" questions. The person conducting the MOT is trying to help the recipient discover what is happening and what the root cause is in step two. Once we get to the root cause of the issue, we can move into step three.

MOT Step 3

Step three is coming up with a plan of action to help them get back inside the Freedom V and stay there. In the case of being late, maybe we have them meet you at work half an hour early each day for a week. If it turned out that it is a deeper issue, maybe it would be a plan for counseling. Helping them build the structure they need to be successful is what this is all about. Structure demands behavior. A good SMART goal will help us create the clear expectations and consequences for the new plan. It is very helpful to have a plan of action in writing. This will help prevent any miscommunication between the two parties. All of this will then lead to the final step of giving feedback.

MOT Step 4

The fourth and final step is feedback. We want to have a structure in place that helps us know whether or not we have completed the plan of action to standard or not. This will be another meeting where we can sit down and communicate. We can see how we did with the plan of action and whether or not we are back to being self-governed.

If we do a MOT after one occurrence of a missed expectation, we sometimes find out that something out of the ordinary has happened. For instance, if someone shows up late one day and we decide to do a MOT with them we may find out that they had a death in the family. That would cause the MOT to terminate immediately. We would move from more results-oriented to relationship-oriented in that moment.

The Four Squares

When conducting a MOT we can use the Four Squares to assist us in helping others realize what they are doing. There are only four reasons people do or do not do something. It is all about ability and motivation. They either can't and won't (no ability or desire), can't but want to (no ability but have the desire), can but won't (have the ability but not the motivation) or they can and will (have the ability and desire). Generally, for a MOT people are in the "can but won't" square. Helping them see this can be very eye opening.

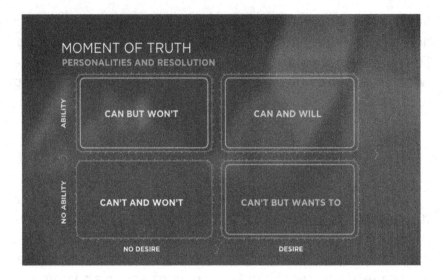

Four Squares Example

After you complete step one and they acknowledge the reality that they are not doing what is expected of them and you get the story, you simply show the chart above and ask them what square they are in. Typically they will point to "can and will" and say, "I can be in this one." You both know they can and appreciate the thought, so you might say, "I agree, but which square are you in right now? Please touch it." Getting them to put their finger in the "can but won't" square can be very eye opening for people. Having to actually physically touch the square to admit that they are trained to do the task and are choosing to not do it, creates a much deeper realization. They then need to understand that we expect them to be in the "can and will" box immediately. If they continue in the "can but won't" box, they will not be able to continue to be a member of the team any longer. This helps in creating and solidifying a plan and structure to get them where they need to be so they can be successful. If during this process it's determined that that they are in the "can't but want to" square, this is a function of not being trained properly and the MOT should end. We can't have expectations for people to complete tasks that they do not have any idea how to do. Having a "can't but want to" person is a great opportunity to exercise Expert Power through Participative or Delegating Leadership to get them trained.

There may be times where someone has to have a MOT about which square they are touching. If they point to the "can't but want to" square but you know they are trained, you may have to dig deeper into the MOT process to help them see that they have been trained and it is actually a motivation issue. This is not very normal in a culture that shares truth often but it does happen frequently in cultures where sharing truth is used as a tool to break people down instead of using truth to serve them. Truth-less cultures will have created a climate of insecurity and defensiveness where making mistakes is not seen as an opportunity to learn and grow but are intolerable. Cultures in learning organizations, relationships and families embrace honest mistakes as wonderful opportunities to mentor and execute the Act/Learn/Adjust (ALA) process. They share truth with grace and mercy through asking questions and influencing others to self-discovery learning. These cultures execute forgiveness for mistakes and use those mistakes as learning points and do not hold them over the heads of others.

Matthew 6: 14-15

"For if you forgive men their trespasses, your heavenly Father will also forgive you. But if you do not forgive men their trespasses, neither will your Father forgive your trespasses.-NKJV

In the scripture reading above, Jesus is telling us that we are given a lot of grace and mercy for forgiveness of our mistakes. Many of us have people in our lives that will grant grace and mercy through forgiveness over and over again. We enjoy the fact that we are allowed to make mistakes and learn lessons. However, we often find ourselves not granting the same grace and mercy to others as God has provided us. The Me THERE says that grace and mercy are good and deserved by me but others don't deserve the same.

How many chances should we give others? When someone is making mistakes all of the time, how many MOTs should we have before we separate them from the team? The answer is found in Jesus' words above. We should give them as many chances as we would want to have. We will all be judged by the same measuring stick we use to judge others. Or as a close friend of mine, Clif Coleman, says, "It's a short trip from one side of the desk to the other."

How do you view the intentional mistakes of someone who purposefully violates the boundaries of the Freedom V? Once the MOT is complete, do you forgive them? Do you give them a fresh start or are you waiting for them to make the next mistake to deliver justice? What does it mean to truly forgive someone else? To truly forgive their mistakes, you have to not use their past transgressions against them in thought, word or deed.

At some point, we may need to ask someone to leave the team. After numerous MOTs or intentional violations of the boundaries for their Freedom V, it may come to the point of having to separate them from the team. This can be in a way that also serves them. When separating them from the team, we can do this in a MOT process that will hopefully give them the "aha moment" required for them to change their ways. This last effort may cause them to go to their next team with a different attitude or different actions.

Organizations who measure small and measure often will share truth as part of who they are and how they execute their normal daily routine. When they do this, MOT naturally happens. In most cases, it will be a simple sarcastic remark or funny jab to let the other person know that they are accountable. These are in the minor infractions. These take place in the hallways and breakrooms and not in formal settings. Just ribbing each other or making the funny, snarky remark can be effective in these cultures to help the other person be accountable. Even peers may use it to help with accountability and it promotes self-governance. You may see one person say sarcastically or jokingly, "You must keep getting a flat tire for the past two days to walk through the door five minutes late." The other person may reply with, "Yep, got caught in traffic." That gives the first person the opportunity to ask, "What square are you in?" At this point both people have seen an MOT done many times and know the four squares tool. They will both laugh but the point has been taken. That is usually all it takes to help them rethink their position. They have done a mini-MOT and it was effective. This can only work in organizations where truth is part of who you are and what you do. It will not work in organizations that don't measure small and measure often.

2 Samuel 11, 12: 1-15

It happened in the spring of the year, at the time when kings go out *to battle,* that David sent Joab and his servants with him, and all Israel; and they destroyed the people of Ammon and besieged Rabbah. But David remained at Jerusalem.

Then it happened one evening that David arose from his bed and walked on the roof of the king's house. And from the roof he saw a woman bathing, and the woman *was* very beautiful to behold. So David sent and inquired about the woman. And *someone* said, "*Is* this not Bathsheba, the daughter of Eliam, the wife of Uriah the Hittite?" Then David sent messengers, and took her; and she came to him, and he lay with her, for she was cleansed from her impurity; and she returned to her house. And the woman conceived; so she sent and told David, and said, "I *am* with child."

Then David sent to Joab, *saying,* "Send me Uriah the Hittite." And Joab sent Uriah to David. When Uriah had come to him, David asked how Joab was doing, and how the people were doing, and how the war prospered. And David said to Uriah, "Go down to your house and wash your feet." So Uriah departed from the king's house, and a gift *of food* from the king followed him. But Uriah slept at the door of the king's house with all the servants of his lord, and did not go down to his house. So when they told David, saying, "Uriah did not go down to his house," David said to Uriah, "Did you not come from a journey? Why did you not go down to your house?"

And Uriah said to David, "The ark and Israel and Judah are dwelling in tents, and my lord Joab and the servants of my lord are encamped in the open fields. Shall I then go to my house to eat and drink, and to lie with my wife? *As* you live, and *as* your soul lives, I will not do this thing."

Then David said to Uriah, "Wait here today also, and tomorrow I will let you depart." So Uriah remained in Jerusalem that day and the next. Now when David called him, he ate and drank before him; and he made him drunk. And at evening he went out to lie on his bed with the servants of his lord, but he did not go down to his house.

In the morning it happened that David wrote a letter to Joab and sent *it* by the hand of Uriah. And he wrote in the letter, saying, "Set Uriah in the forefront of the hottest battle, and retreat from him, that he may be struck down and die." So it was, while Joab besieged the city, that he assigned Uriah to a place where he knew there *were* valiant men. Then the men of the city came out and fought with Joab. And *some* of the people of the servants of David fell; and Uriah the Hittite died also.

Then Joab sent and told David all the things concerning the war, and charged the messenger, saying, "When you have finished telling the matters of the war to the king, if it happens that the king's wrath rises, and he says to you:

'Why did you approach so near to the city when you fought? Did you not know that they would shoot from the wall? Who struck Abimelech the son of Jerubbesheth? Was it not a woman who cast a piece of a millstone on him from the wall, so that he died in Thebez? Why did you go near the wall?'—then you shall say, 'Your servant Uriah the Hittite is dead also.'"

So the messenger went, and came and told David all that Joab had sent by him. And the messenger said to David, "Surely the men prevailed against us and came out to us in the field; then we drove them back as far as the entrance of the gate. The archers shot from the wall at your servants; and *some* of the king's servants are dead, and your servant Uriah the Hittite is dead also."

Then David said to the messenger, "Thus you shall say to Joab: 'Do not let this thing displease you, for the sword devours one as well as another. Strengthen your attack against the city, and overthrow it.' So encourage him."

When the wife of Uriah heard that Uriah her husband was dead, she mourned for her husband. And when her mourning was over, David sent and brought her to his house, and she became his wife and bore him a son. But the thing that David had done displeased the LORD.

Then the LORD sent Nathan to David. And he came to him, and said to him: "There were two men in one city, one rich and the other poor. The rich *man* had exceedingly many flocks and herds. But the poor *man* had nothing, except one little ewe lamb which he had bought and nourished; and it grew up together with him and with his children. It ate of his own food and drank from his own cup and lay in his bosom; and it was like a daughter to him. And a traveler came to the rich man, who refused to take from his own flock and from his own herd to prepare one for the wayfaring man who had come to him; but he took the poor man's lamb and prepared it for the man who had come to him."

So David's anger was greatly aroused against the man, and he said to Nathan, *"As* the LORD lives, the man who has done this shall surely die! And he shall restore fourfold for the lamb, because he did this thing and because he had no pity."

Then Nathan said to David, "You *are* the man! Thus says the LORD God of Israel: 'I anointed you king over Israel, and I delivered you from the hand of Saul. I gave you your master's house and your master's wives into your keeping, and gave you the house of Israel and Judah. And if *that had been* too little, I also would have given you much more! Why have you despised the commandment of the LORD, to do evil in His sight? You have killed Uriah the Hittite with the sword; you have taken his wife *to be* your wife, and have killed him with the sword of the people of Ammon. Now therefore, the sword shall never depart from your house, because you have despised Me, and have taken the wife of Uriah the Hittite to be your wife.' Thus says the LORD: 'Behold, I will raise up adversity against you from your own house; and I will take your wives before your eyes and give *them* to your neighbor, and he shall lie with your wives in the sight of this sun. For you did *it* secretly, but I will do this thing before all Israel, before the sun.'"

So David said to Nathan, "I have sinned against the LORD."

And Nathan said to David, "The LORD also has put away your sin; you shall not die. However, because by this deed you have given great occasion to the enemies of the LORD to blaspheme, the child also *who is* born to you shall surely die." Then Nathan departed to his house.-NKJV

From the scripture reading above, we can see how God used the MOT with David. He uses the four-step process in a very artful way. We see King David's sin of having an affair with another woman (Bathsheba) who was married to Uriah. The affair resulted in the conception of a child. In an attempt to cover the sin, David tried to get Uriah to lay with his Bathsheba but was unsuccessful. Instead of confessing his sin, King David took his sin to the next level by ordering the death of Uriah.

God sends the Prophet Nathan in to King David with the story of the sheep that enrages David. David is ready to drop the hammer of justice on the rich man for his transgressions. Nathan tells David that it is him of whom he is speaking. Through the use of a story, David realizes the truth. He says, "I have sinned against the Lord." The depth of the moment of truth was not as simple as having an affair or murder. It was clarified as what it really is, sinning against the Lord. God, through Nathan, has completed step one of the MOT. David sees the truth of his transgressions and knows the story. He is guilty and God passes judgement. The child will not live and the House of David will always know war. This is the plan of action for David to always remember his sins against God. This completes the plan of action for David (step 3). Step four is fulfilled over the rest of David's life with his son Absalom rising against him.

Seeking Truth

We should also seek truth for ourselves. Understanding our own current reality (HERE) is critical to setting an example for others. We should find someone we can trust to share truth with us. A good rule of thumb is to assume all of their observations are true until proven otherwise. This mindset allows us to work on things that we may otherwise dismiss as not true. We tend to think we are much better at things than we really are. Assuming that the person you trust is sharing truth honestly to serve you is a good mindset to have when approaching truth for ourselves. Seeking truth from others requires a tremendous amount of humility and self-awareness.

Resolving Conflict

During the MOT process there is almost always going to be some conflict. This will be more prevalent in cultures that don't embrace truth and the current reality of the HERE. However, conflict doesn't have to be viewed as negative.

Most of the words we think of when we think of conflict are negative. We tend to view conflict as a bad thing. Conflict is all around us, every day. Whenever there is any lack of clarity of the THERE, there will be some conflict. Whenever there is lack of current reality in the HERE, there will be conflict. Whenever we move into the pit of despair, there will be conflict. In other words, conflict will always be present. However, conflict is healthy and can be good. It is how we handle conflict that can be bad.

There are five ways to handle conflict. There is competing, avoiding, accommodating, compromising and collaborating. All five styles of conflict resolution can be good. The problem is that we tend to overuse and underuse some. To handle conflict appropriately, we need to use the appropriate conflict resolution style at the appropriate time. There will be times that a competing style will be necessary and we may inappropriately use avoidance instead. This will only make the conflict worse and prolong the conflict or even destroy the relationship.

Inappropriate use of the conflict resolution styles is the biggest reason people tend to not share truth. When we aren't trained to handle conflict appropriately we tend to avoid it at all costs or we tend to overreact to the situation. Timely and appropriate use of the conflict resolution styles will result in the effective resolution to a MOT.

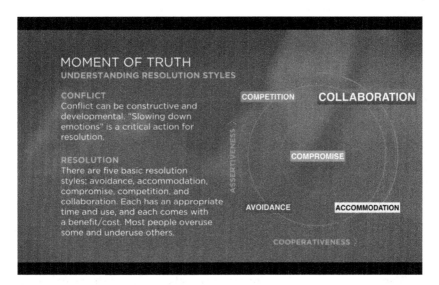

MOMENT OF TRUTH
UNDERSTANDING RESOLUTION STYLES

CONFLICT
Conflict can be constructive and developmental. "Slowing down emotions" is a critical action for resolution.

RESOLUTION
There are five basic resolution styles; avoidance, accommodation, compromise, competition, and collaboration. Each has an appropriate time and use, and each comes with a benefit/cost. Most people overuse some and underuse others.

There are five basic conflict resolution styles; competition, collaboration, compromise, accommodation, and avoidance. We each have a natural bent that we use when we are faced with conflict. Understanding that we tend to lean on and overuse one of the five conflict resolution styles can help us prevent that.

Competition

The first style is competition. When we use this style of conflict resolution, there is a winner and there is a loser (win-lose). For example, let's use our couple from the Project Mood Curve chapter who were struggling with the tooth paste. If you'll recall, he liked Crest and she liked Colgate. He squeezed at the end of the tube and she squeezed in the middle. If they use the competition conflict resolution style, there will be a winner and a loser. It is typically a "my way or the highway" type scenario. If he is competing, there will be no ground given. He will want to have his Crest Toothpaste and squeeze from the end of the tube and not give in.

Accommodation

The opposite of competing is accommodation. When one person is competing and wins, the other is accommodating. This is also a win-lose scenario where one person gets what they want and the other accommodates it. In the toothpaste case, maybe she doesn't care enough about toothpaste or where it is squeezed to want to stand her ground for it so she accommodates.

Compromise

The third conflict resolution style is compromise. In compromising, each person wins a little and loses a little (win-lose, lose-win). In our toothpaste scenario, it would look like he gets Crest but has to squeeze in the middle of the tube. She will have to use Crest but get to squeeze in the middle of the tube. Each person gave something up and got something in return.

Avoidance

Our fourth style of conflict resolution is avoidance. There are often scenarios where we need to use avoidance. When we realize that emotions are running high and nothing we say or do will be impactful at that particular moment, we can take a time out and avoid the situation. With avoidance, we haven't exited the conflict, we have delayed it until we are more prepared mentally and emotionally to deal with it in a healthy way. It is kicking the can down the road. There is no winner and no loser. In our toothpaste scenario, she may decide that his emotions are way too high for him to see logic and decide to avoid the conversation until things settle down.

Collaborating

The fifth conflict resolution style is collaborating. In collaboration we have a win-win. Both parties get what they want. Here our happy couple may decide that they both like Aim Toothpaste as much as they like Crest or Colgate. They also both like the pump-style toothpaste so they don't have to squeeze the tube at all. They have both won. Collaboration often yields the best results but it can be very difficult to achieve.

A conflict may not start and end with the same resolution style. You may cycle through all of the conflict resolution styles during one discussion. You may start competing and realize that the other person who is also competing has a better idea than you. At this point you may shift into accommodating. Or if their idea has some good points but so does yours, you may compromise. This could also lead to a collaboration. Finally, if emotions are running high and there is nothing to be gained by continuing the discussion you could avoid it for now.

The importance of this is to just be aware of which style you are using and why. We should always compete when our values are concerned. However, some of us like to compete on every little item. You may have heard the phrase about picking your battles. People who only compete pick every battle. They can be looked at as argumentative and ultimately may get left out of some important conversations because they will only stand on what they think. The same is true with the other conflict resolution styles. When we over use or under use one too many times, we can lose our effectiveness.

Many people who over use the avoidance conflict resolution style go through a cycle of avoidance that can result in passive-aggressive actions. They can also follow a cycle of not wanting to upset the apple cart so they don't say anything. Then the other person or people continue with their behavior that is bothering us. We decide not to say anything again. This goes on for a period until it gets to the point where we become extremely emotional and we erupt like an emotional volcano. Everyone around us is shocked by the outburst because we never said anything about the actions bothering us prior.

A MOT can also be done when someone does something well. When they don't recognize that they had a large part in achieving something, you can help them see that they did with a MOT. This, unfortunately, is not a very normal occurrence. Generally, people see their role and have an inflated opinion of what it was to the team.

The key to preventing the emotions from getting the best of us is to simply measure small and measure often. When we share truth in this way, we are serving others and helping them improve. We are loving them more than ourselves. Truth is foundational to great organizations, families and relationships. Without truth these entities flounder and fail. We should share this truth with mercy and grace. We can use the Moment of Truth to help us do this.

CHAPTER 7

Handling Emotions/Systems Thinking

(HERE Tool #5)

Proverbs 16: 32
He who is slow to anger is better than the mighty and he who rules his spirit than he who takes a city-NKJV

Emotions come from our overarching thinking. They come from what we will introduce later as our System 1 Thinking. These emotions are not good or bad. We are having them for a reason. The way we process emotions and act on them can be good or bad. However, emotions are responders and often untrustworthy. Emotions are reactions to an external stimulus but they, in and of themselves, are not to be trusted.

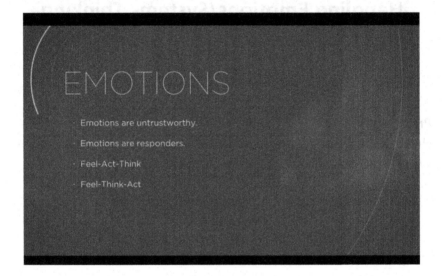

Dealing with emotions

We can choose how to deal with our emotions. We can choose to control our emotions or have our emotions control us. When the emotion hits, we can Feel-Think-Act or we can Feel-Act-Think. That is our choice. We can feel the emotion, and slow down our emotions and then act. This takes self-governance and practice. You normally feel the surge of emotions with an uptick in blood pressure, increased heart rate and flushing of your face.

When we feel this take place, we can think before we act. This may look like avoiding the conflict for a time, taking a time out, taking a deep breath or counting to ten. There are numerous techniques for slowing down our emotions. However, it takes a conscious effort to slow them down. You can feel the surge of emotions and understand that they are telling you an action is required. Next, you can say, "Thank you emotions, I will take it from here." Now that you have recognized you are experiencing an emotion and why, you can act under good cognitive judgement rather than reflexive response.

If we choose to Feel-Act-Think, we usually find out that emotions beget emotions. When we respond reflexively while being emotion-led, it usually introduces more emotion into the other person or people. This circle of emotions can continue to build until it becomes destructive. There are many techniques we can use to slow our emotions down. A good one to use during conflict or argument is to simply ask questions. This causes you to slow down your emotions and think about what to ask as well as cause the other person to slow his down to think about a response.

There are many different techniques we can use to slow our emotions. The key is to first recognize what is happening. It takes a great deal of practice. When we recognize that emotions are hitting us, we can use these techniques to distance ourselves from the situation and try to figure out how we can best serve the other person in the situation.

Negative emotions like loneliness, envy, and guilt have an important role to play in a happy life; they're big, flashing signs that something needs to change.-Gretchen Rubin

Systems Thinking

Now that we know our emotions come from our overarching thinking, let's examine the human mind. The human mind operates on three systems of thinking that have cleverly been named system one, system two and system three.

System 1

System one thinking is the patterned thinking our brain does automatically. Should you approach or retreat? Should you duck or jump? The human mind acts instinctively because of past experiences. We can develop a very accurate and sophisticated system one thought process over time. However, our system one is influenced by emotions and heuristics. Heuristics are mental short cuts or biases. For most of us, driving is a system one function. Have you ever gone through a stop sign without remembering it? You just go into autopilot and your system one takes over reflexively. A close friend told me when describing System 1 to his mother, he asked her if she knew how many stop signs she went through from the house to work. She couldn't. She had to concentrate and count. It was three. And she makes the drive twice every single day.

In the military, we trained for thousands of hours on how to react to battlefield situations. We would train these situations so many times that they would become muscle memory. They would become system one. The military calls these situations battle drills. When an enemy fires a shot at the unit, the unit executes the react to contact battle drill. They immediately get down, find cover, return fire and communicate the direction and distance to the enemy position. This is trained so much it becomes an immediate reaction to this situation. That is how system one works. It is an instinctive reaction to something in the environment.

Here is another way we find our system one thinking take over:

Imagine you are at a baseball field near a school and the workers uncover some stone with fossil footprints embedded into it (as shown below). As they uncover it in thirds, you are asked by the teacher, "What happened here?"

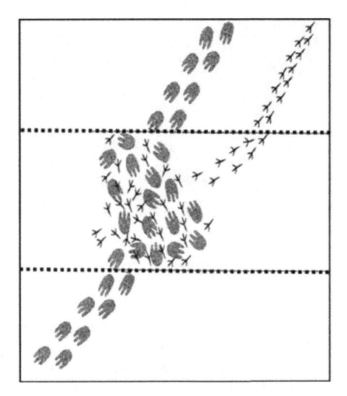

You probably came up with a pretty good story for what happened. Maybe you said that a bird and a bear got into a fight and the bear ate the bird. Or maybe the bird flew away. The system one mind fills in blanks with opinions and assumptions and then turns them into a story just like you did here.

System 1- The Human Mind
- Sees Data
- Turns the Data into a Story
- Fills in gaps with assumptions and speculations
- The assumptions and speculations are influenced by emotions and heuristics
- This all happens automatically

System 2

System two is the focused human mind. It blocks out the outside distractions and filters out the emotions and heuristics simply by recognizing which ones are present and setting them aside. Continued proper use of the system two thinking will influence and develop a better system one.

System 2- The Focused Human Mind
- Recognizes the Process of System 1
- Recognizes potential emotions and heuristics involved (affecting assumptions)
- Decides which assumptions to believe
- Decides which patterns to follow

When we get into trouble or action needs to be taken, we can use our system one, or if time permits, shift into system two. Shifting into system two more often will help develop the system one to a point that when we need to use system one, it will be a better, more appropriate response. Even learning to drive a car in the system one example required a great deal of system two initially. When you first got behind the wheel, you were probably very focused on the yellow line, where your hands were placed, how deliberate you were in checking the mirrors and you probably had to shut off the radio or block it out to get the focus you needed just to stay in the lines. You did this often enough that now you don't really even think about it anymore. It is just instinctive. Your continued and constant appropriate use of system two resulted in a highly refined system one for driving a car.

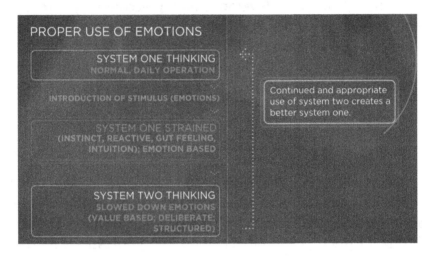

There has been a great deal of research done on the systems thinking. System one can be developed and honed to the point of great accuracy. There are people who have studied tennis matches so much that they can tell you with 95% accuracy if the ball is going in or out before it even touches the racket. There are art dealers who have studied art so much that they can tell you if something is a fake or not just by glancing at it. They may not know why they know but their gut instinct (system one) is telling them it is.

System one can be developed through experience or through shifting into system two more frequently. You may have heard about the 10,000 hours required to become an expert at something. Life experience over the course of decades allows us a more enhanced system one because we have experienced things many times over. Our system one knows what to expect. As we get older, we tend to have a better or more refined system one in the areas of our lives that we work and live. The experts would say this 10,000 hours of repetitive experience is required to make a highly developed system one. The only way to shortcut this is to shift into system two. Shifting into system two where you are focused on the task, and nothing else, can allow us to shortcut that time in some instances.

Although we can develop a highly accurate system one with time and practice, it is still influenced by emotions and heuristics. We all know the emotions can influence but let's take a look at some of the heuristics that can affect our system one and cause us to get it wrong.

Heuristics

Daniel Kahneman conducted extensive research on heuristics or biases and documented dozens of them in his book *Thinking Fast and Slow.* One heuristic he talks about is the Halo Effect. This is where good first impressions tend to positively color later negative impressions and vice versa. The first to speak their opinion at a meeting will set the tone for the meeting and cause it to go positive or negative.

Another is heuristic is Anchoring. You have this happen to you when you are driving through town and then get out onto the freeway. You feel like you are driving faster than you should. The same happens coming off the freeway and then going into town. You may find yourself speeding because it feels like you are driving too slowly.

A third heuristic is the Law of Small Numbers. Our brains have a difficult time with statistics. Small samples are prone to more extreme outcomes than large samples, but we lend the outcome from the smaller samples more credence than statistics warrant. System one is impressed with the outcome of small samples but shouldn't be.

A fourth heuristic is Representativeness. This is the physical pillar. When someone or something looks the part, we grant it a higher degree of effectiveness. Baseball scouts used to recruit players based on how close their appearance resembled other good players.

A fifth heuristic is the Sunk Cost Fallacy. To avoid feeling bad about cutting our losses and being a failure, we tend to throw good money after bad. We may stay too long in an unfulfilling career or abusive marriages because we have invested so much. This is optimism gone hay wire.

There are several more heuristics but the final one we will investigate is priming. Priming is one of the major heuristics that we fall prey to. One way we see priming is when we read about old people, we tend to walk slower. Let's take a deeper look at how this works by taking a short quiz adopted from a TED Talk by Hans Rosling. Answer each question without thinking too hard about it. Use your system one instinctive response to answer quickly.

1) Globally, how did deaths per year from natural disaster change in the last century?
   a. more than doubled
   b. remained the same
   c. decreased to less than half

2) In the last 20 years the percentage of people in the world in extreme poverty has:
   a. Almost doubled
   b. Remained the same
   c. Almost halved

3) What percentage of the world's 1 year olds are vaccinated against measles?
   a. 20%
   b. 50%
   c. 80%

Answers: In 1900 half a million people a year died from natural disaster and now less that two hundred thousand die a year. The answer to number one is C. Less than twelve percent of Americans answered the question correctly. The answer to number two is also C. Less than five percent of Americans answered that one correctly. The answer to number three is also C. Less than seventeen percent of Americans answered this one correctly as well. How can this be? How can we not even beat the odds of guessing with a 33% chance of guessing correctly? The answer is that we are influenced by the Priming heuristic every day. The news media reports on these subjects so much that we begin to see them as bigger issues than they really are. Here are some other fun facts:

Your chances of being killed by a shark, 1/3.7 million, is less than being killed by an elephant.

You have a better chance of being killed by fireworks (1/340,000) or struck by lightning (1/~80,000) than killed in a terrorist attack.

Only relying on system one can cause us to get it wrong. System one is a good thing but it is influenced by emotions and the heuristics that are always around us.

When I began my last assignment in the Army, I was responsible for an organization of around 900 personnel. I had over twenty years experience learning and understanding people. I had experienced people from every walk of life for over two decades. My system one on what they need to get to the THERE was very refined. I was probably getting it right 98% of the time.

My first weekend in my new position I had a young man get arrested for driving under the influence of alcohol. Getting arrested for DUI in the Army is a pretty big deal and I was required to personally speak with the young man and his chain of command on their weekend off.

I brought the soldier and his leadership in on that Saturday morning and asked him what happened. I could see from his body language, tears in his eyes and shaking voice that by the end of our conversation he understood the gravity of the situation. My system one told me that this was just a case of a young man going out on a Friday night with no plan and partying too hard. After admonishing him, I told his chain of command to make sure he knew that he could recover from this but he would lose his driving privileges on post.

That night the young man went home, got up in the middle of the night and hung himself in his laundry room with an extension cord. I had made a terrible mistake. I had relied on my system one thinking when dealing with his situation and it was wrong. This was not a case of partying too hard. This was a case of something much deeper. He was experiencing a great deal of PTSD and the DUI was a symptom of the problem and not the problem itself. I thought I knew what he needed and didn't investigate further by shifting into system two.

I don't blame myself for his death. That was a choice he made. However, had I taken the time to shift into system two, I may have discovered what was really going on in his life and prevented his death. My system one had failed me and this became a huge turning point in my life. I learned that whenever I have the time, I need to shift into system two.

System 3

System three thinking is listening through prayer. It is listening to the Holy Spirit. This results in a renewed mind. System three is about serving others and it is about finding truth. When we base our decisions off of truth, God's truth, instead of what we have as our cultural or societal "truths", we can start to see things through the proper lens.

System one is good. It is all about the body. It is there to help us make split-second decisions that keep us from getting hurt. System two is better but not as quick. It is the voice in our head that is our conscience. It helps us determine what is legally right and wrong by setting aside the heuristics and emotions it recognizes. System three is the best. System one and two are self-serving. System three is serving others. System three filters our thoughts through the Word to find Truth. It helps us make decisions based on what is best to serve God and to serve others instead of ourselves.

System 3- Our Spiritual Selves

- The voices in our head help us make decisions
  - System 1 is based on experience but influenced by emotions and heuristics
  - System 2 is deeper thought that lays aside these emotions and heuristics but still self-serving

- System 3 is listening to the Holy Spirit
- System 3 is listening through Prayer

- System 3 is filtering our thoughts through The Word
  - What is truth? What does The Word say?

- System 3 allows us to make choices with our renewed mind and is not self-serving

Ephesians 4: 17-24

This I say, therefore, and testify in the Lord, that you should no longer walk as the rest of the Gentiles walk, in the futility of their mind, having their understanding darkened, being alienated from the life of God, because of the ignorance that is in them, because of the blindness of their heart; who, being past feeling, have given themselves over to lewdness, to work all uncleanness with greediness.

But you have not so learned Christ, if indeed you have heard Him and have been taught by Him, as the truth is in Jesus: that you put off, concerning your former conduct, the old man which grows corrupt according to the deceitful lusts, and be renewed in the spirit of your mind, and that you put on the new man which was created according to God, in true righteousness and holiness.-NKJV

Continued habitual use of system three will result in a more developed system one that will automatically serve others. This is the renewed mind. When our first thoughts are about others rather than ourselves we will have reached this renewed mind. This is a transcendent THERE for us. We will always struggle with serving ME vs serving WE but we are given the opportunity to walk in the Spirit and have life or choose to walk in the flesh and face death.

1 Corinthians 2: 1-16

And I, brethren, when I came to you, did not come with excellence of speech or of wisdom declaring to you the testimony of God. For I determined not to know anything among you except Jesus Christ and Him crucified. I was with you in weakness, in fear, and in much trembling. And my speech and my preaching *were* not with persuasive words of human wisdom, but in demonstration of the Spirit and of power, that your faith should not be in the wisdom of men but in the power of God.

However, we speak wisdom among those who are mature, yet not the wisdom of this age, nor of the rulers of this age, who are coming to nothing. But we speak the wisdom of God in a mystery, the hidden *wisdom* which God ordained before the ages for our glory, which none of the rulers of this age knew; for had they known, they would not have crucified the Lord of glory.

But as it is written: "Eye has not seen, nor ear heard, nor have entered into the heart of man the things which God has prepared for those who love Him."

But God has revealed *them* to us through His Spirit. For the Spirit searches all things, yes, the deep things of God. For what man knows the things of a man except the spirit of the man which is in him? Even so no one knows the things of God except the Spirit of God. Now we have received, not the spirit of the world, but the Spirit who is from God, that we might know the things that have been freely given to us by God.

These things we also speak, not in words which man's wisdom teaches but which the Holy Spirit teaches, comparing spiritual things with spiritual. But the natural man does not receive the things of the Spirit of God, for they are foolishness to him; nor can he know *them,* because they are spiritually discerned. But he who is spiritual judges all things, yet he himself is *rightly* judged by no one. For "who has known the mind of the LORD that he may instruct Him?" But we have the mind of Christ.-NKJV

Romans 12: 1-2

I beseech you therefore, brethren, by the mercies of God, that you present your bodies a living sacrifice, holy, acceptable to God, *which is* your reasonable service. And do not be conformed to this world, but be transformed by the renewing of your mind, that you may prove what *is* that good and acceptable and perfect will of God.

In the scripture readings above, Paul talks about the mind of Christ. He talks about having this renewed mind. This mind through the Holy Spirit is the system three mind. It is the renewed mind that Paul struggled to achieve throughout his time spreading the word of Christ. System three is something we will always have to work at and is more of a Transcendent THERE than something achievable at all times.

*Depiction of Washington by John Trumbull

Thinking back to the story of George Washington and the Newburgh Address, which systems thinking did he use? He decided to shift into system two and give himself five days to write a speech and talk to others. However, we know George Washington was a pious man. He would have asked God for his guidance. God used George Washington's physical frailty and humility to serve others rather than use his words. This happened through the renewed mind. He undoubtedly shifted into system three thinking. What was in his heart came through to change the minds of others.

Our overarching thinking that stems from system one determines which emotions we will have to deal with and how intense these emotions will be. We can change our system one thinking by utilizing system three. This undoubtedly will eliminate some of the negative emotions that come our way. However, no matter how hard we try we will always have to deal with emotions. We don't want to be emotionless but we don't want to be led by our emotions either. When dealing with those emotions, we can Feel-Act-Think or we can Feel-Think-Act. Choosing to Feel-Think-Act prevents being emotion led.

We have to keep in mind that these emotions are responding to an external stimulus and just telling us something needs to be addressed. We can choose to act on that or we can slow our emotions down and then act.

We usually see emotions flare when our HERE enters the pit of despair along the PATH. While in the pit of despair, we are normally in the storming phase of team development and people may not have clarity of their roles. This causes people to step outside the structure of their Freedom V and forces their leaders to do a MOT. When doing the MOT, there will usually be a level of conflict that will cause some emotions. Utilizing the emotions tool can help you have a better reaction that serves others towards your THERE rather than serving yourself.

"You may not be able to control your circumstances but you can control your responses"-Foster Friess

The Essex

The Essex is the American whaling ship the book Moby Dick is based on. In 1820, the Essex was 2,000 miles West of South America in the prime whale hunting grounds when they were struck by a large sperm whale. The whale had struck the ship hard enough to cause it to sink. The men gathered what supplies they could salvage prior to boarding the whale boats and abandoning the area.

The closest islands were the Marquesas Islands and they were 1200 miles away. The crew had inadequate supplies of food and water to reach them. Captain Pollard feared setting sail for the Marquesas Islands because he thought them inhabited by cannibals. Instead of shifting into System Two thinking, the captain and crew decided to head towards

South America which would be a 3,000 mile journey due to the trade winds. They didn't consider the probable death of starvation and dehydration due to the emotions of fear influencing their thought processes.

Around forty days into the voyage, the crewmen began to die one by one. At first, the crewmen sewed the bodies into their clothes and buried them at sea. Soon it became obvious that they would all perish if they didn't find a food source and they began to resort to cannibalism. They resorted to doing exactly what they had feared. They began eating the dead crewmen.

Many of the boats had become separated in a squall and continued the journey alone. Several months into the voyage, some of the crew survived through being picked up by passing ships or rescued from remote islands. Throughout his career, Captain Pollard would go on to captain a few more ships through the years that all sank until no one would fund him anymore due to him being so unlucky.

When making decisions, we should use our systems thinking properly and slow down emotions where possible. If the crew had set aside their fears, they may have all survived. Instead, their emotions ruled their thoughts and they never took the time to shift into System Two thinking. Slowing down when possible and recognizing which emotions and heuristics are at work would have helped their situation considerably. But shifting into System Three and listening to the Holy Spirit results in the best decisions for others.

CHAPTER 8

The Two Circles

(HERE Tool #6)

We are not born a winner or a loser. However, we are born a chooser.

Have you ever had someone cut you off in traffic? Has anyone ever challenged your authority? Have you ever been fired from a job? Have you ever had anything bad happen to you?

When something unexpectedly bad happens to us, we tend to find ourselves playing the role of the victim.

The Hapless Bartender

On February 12th 1809 a boy was born to two loving parents on the frontier of Kentucky. His family moved to Indiana when he was very young. When he was nine years old, his mother passed away. The young boy took her death pretty hard. He was raised by his father and eleven year old sister.

The boy loved to read. Books were hard to come by in rural Indiana but he managed to track some down and became self-educated. As a teenager, his family moved to Illinois where he continued his love of reading and education. He was doing very well for himself as a young man and decided to go into business with a partner in a tavern.

The young man was only a minority partner in the tavern and after a few weeks of bartending, he decided that this life was not for him. He let his partner buy him out and decided to move on with life.

Shortly after leaving the partnership, our hapless bartender was called into court. His old partner had evidently faulted on some debts. The judge told the young bartender that he was responsible for a sizable portion of the debt. The hapless bartender argued his case to the judge. He stated that he was only a partner for a couple weeks and no longer had anything to do with the business. The judge didn't see it his way and ordered him to pay the debt.

The debt was a very sizable one. The courts seized his horse, house and most of his personal possessions to pay it off. Our hapless bartender had to be feeling pretty bad about this time. How could this be happening to him? This wasn't fair! It wasn't his fault! How could this be any part of God's plan? **He was in the Victim Circle.**

He was able to borrow money from a number of close friends and get back most of his stuff. The young man counted his blessings and vowed never to get into the tavern business ever again. Six short months later he was called back into court. His old business partner had died and was in a tremendous amount of debt.

The judge ordered our hapless bartender to pay the full debt for his deceased partner. The young man argued vehemently that he was not even an interest owner in the tavern. He should have nothing to do with this debt. This was unfair! The judge told him that if he wanted to stay out of trouble, he should study the law. He should attend law school and learn not to get himself into bad business arrangements.

Defeated, our hapless bartender decided to do just what the judge suggested. He picked up some law books and passed the Bar to become an attorney in Illinois in just under two years. As it turned out, he was a pretty good lawyer.

In 1846 he was elected to the Illinois House of representatives and in 1860 he became the President of the United States. You see, Abraham Lincoln did not know why he was being forced to pay those fines. He originally went into the Victim Circle and then decided that God had him where he wanted him for a reason. He had a choice. He chose to move into the Choice Circle and affect his life, the people around him and his circumstances. Had he not found himself in a poor business relationship or had he decided to remain a victim, history would have been very different.

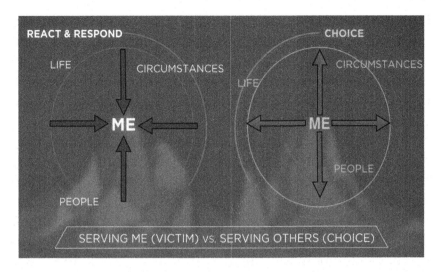

The Victim Circle, above on the left, is where we can find ourselves when we get hit with emotions. We immediately make it all about ME. The arrows all point inward towards ME. Life, people and circumstances are happening to *me*. This circle is all react and respond. We have to slow our emotions down (feel-think-act) and realize that we do have a choice. We always have a choice.

The circle on the right is the circle of choice. This is where we want to be because is me affecting my life, influencing people, and circumstances. I have a choice. I always have choice. This is difficult to remember and stopping yourself from going down deep into the victim circle is as easy as recognizing that the choice is present.

When we think back to the chapter on Freedom vs Control, we know that we can always control three things; whom we trust, our perspective and our actions. The two circles is how you control your perspective. I can look at the circumstances I'm going through as a learning opportunity that God has given me or I can look at it through the lens of a victim. Either way it is a choice.

This is a great tool to help yourself understand your current reality (HERE). You can also use this to share truth with others. Do you know someone who spends most of their time in the Victim Circle? Sometimes just realizing what you are doing is enough to get you to choose differently. Once you have taught others this tool, it is easy to do a mini-MOT by just asking, "What circle are you in right now?" People who understand the tool immediately have the realization of what they are doing to themselves.

The Victim Circle can be addicting to some people. They get a lot of attention with the "poor me" routine. They may be there more often than not. Sharing that truth with them can affect change.

There has been a tremendous amount of research done on positivity. Choosing to be positive and look at things as teachable moments rather than negative moments, is life changing. People who are positive tend to be happier, live longer and be healthier. Recognizing that this is a choice we all have is the first step.

The Book of Jonah

Now the word of the LORD came to Jonah the son of Amittai, saying, "Arise, go to Nineveh, that great city, and cry out against it; for their wickedness has come up before Me." But Jonah arose to flee to Tarshish from the presence of the LORD. He went down to Joppa, and found a ship going to Tarshish; so he paid the fare, and went down into it, to go with them to Tarshish from the presence of the LORD.

But the LORD sent out a great wind on the sea, and there was a mighty tempest on the sea, so that the ship was about to be broken up.

Then the mariners were afraid; and every man cried out to his god, and threw the cargo that *was* in the ship into the sea, to lighten the load. But Jonah had gone down into the lowest parts of the ship, had lain down, and was fast asleep.

So the captain came to him, and said to him, "What do you mean, sleeper? Arise, call on your God; perhaps your God will consider us, so that we may not perish."

And they said to one another, "Come, let us cast lots that we may know for whose cause this trouble *has come* upon us." So they cast lots, and the lot fell on Jonah. Then they said to him, "Please tell us! For whose cause *is* this trouble upon us? What is your occupation? And where do you come from? What is your country? And of what people are you?"

So he said to them, "I *am* a Hebrew; and I fear the LORD, the God of heaven, who made the sea and the dry *land.*"

Then the men were exceedingly afraid, and said to him, "Why have you done this?" For the men knew that he fled from the presence of the LORD, because he had told them. Then they said to him, "What shall we do to you that the sea may be calm for us?"—for the sea was growing more tempestuous.

And he said to them, "Pick me up and throw me into the sea; then the sea will become calm for you. For I know that this great tempest *is* because of me."

Nevertheless the men rowed hard to return to land, but they could not, for the sea continued to grow more tempestuous against them. Therefore they cried out to the LORD and said, "We pray, O LORD, please do not let us perish for this man's life, and do not charge us with innocent blood; for You, O LORD, have done as it pleased You." So they picked up Jonah and threw him into the sea, and the sea ceased from its raging. Then the men feared the LORD exceedingly, and offered a sacrifice to the LORD and took vows.

Now the LORD had prepared a great fish to swallow Jonah. And Jonah was in the belly of the fish three days and three nights.

Then Jonah prayed to the LORD his God from the fish's belly. And he said: "I cried out to the LORD because of my affliction, And He answered me. "Out of the belly of Sheol I cried, *And* You heard my voice. For You cast me into the deep, Into the heart of the seas, And the floods surrounded me; All Your billows and Your waves passed over me. Then I said, 'I have been cast out of Your sight; Yet I will look again toward Your holy temple.' The waters surrounded me, *even* to my soul; the deep closed around me; weeds were wrapped around my head. I went down to the moorings of the mountains; the earth with its bars *closed* behind me forever; yet You have brought up my life from the pit, O LORD, my God. "When my soul fainted within me, I remembered the LORD; and my prayer went *up* to You, Into Your holy temple. "Those who regard worthless idols forsake their own Mercy. But I will sacrifice to You with the voice of thanksgiving; I will pay what I have vowed. Salvation *is* of the LORD."

So the LORD spoke to the fish, and it vomited Jonah onto dry *land.*

Now the word of the LORD came to Jonah the second time, saying, "Arise, go to Nineveh, that great city, and preach to it the message that I tell you." So Jonah arose and went to Nineveh, according to the word of the LORD. Now Nineveh was an exceedingly great city, a three-day journey *in extent.* And Jonah began to enter the city on the first day's walk. Then he cried out and said, "Yet forty days, and Nineveh shall be overthrown!"

So the people of Nineveh believed God, proclaimed a fast, and put on sackcloth, from the greatest to the least of them. Then word came to the king of Nineveh; and he arose from his throne and laid aside his robe, covered *himself* with sackcloth and sat in ashes. And he caused *it* to be proclaimed and published throughout Nineveh by the decree of the king and his nobles, saying, let neither man nor beast, herd nor flock, taste anything; do not let them eat, or drink water. But let man and beast be covered with sackcloth, and cry mightily to God; yes, let everyone turn from his evil way and from the violence that is in his hands. Who can tell *if* God will turn and relent, and turn away from His fierce anger, so that we may not perish?

Then God saw their works and that they turned from their evil way; and God relented from the disaster that He had said He would bring upon them, and He did not do it.

But it displeased Jonah exceedingly, and he became angry. So he prayed to the LORD, and said, "Ah, LORD, was not this what I said when I was still in my country? Therefore I fled previously to Tarshish; for I know that You *are* a gracious and merciful God, slow to anger and abundant in lovingkindness, One who relents from doing harm. Therefore now, O LORD, please take my life from me, for *it is* better for me to die than to live!"

Then the LORD said, *"Is it* right for you to be angry?"

So Jonah went out of the city and sat on the east side of the city. There he made himself a shelter and sat under it in the shade, till he might see what would become of the city. And the LORD God prepared a plant and made it come up over Jonah, that it might be shade for his head to deliver him from his misery. So Jonah was very grateful for the plant. But as morning dawned the next day God prepared a worm, and it *so* damaged the plant that it withered. And it happened, when the sun arose, that God prepared a vehement east wind; and the sun beat on Jonah's head, so that he grew faint. Then he wished death for himself, and said, *"It is* better for me to die than to live."

Then God said to Jonah, *"Is it* right for you to be angry about the plant?"

And he said, *"It is* right for me to be angry, even to death!"

But the LORD said, "You have had pity on the plant for which you have not labored, nor made it grow, which came up in a night and perished in a night. And should I not pity Nineveh, that great city, in which are more than one hundred and twenty thousand persons who cannot discern between their right hand and their left—and much livestock?"-NKJV

In the scripture reading above, we can see that Jonah spends most of his time in the Victim Circle. He fears going to Nineveh and tries to hide from God. He demonstrates the victim mentality by running away. While on the ship, he again plays the victim and tells the sailors to throw him overboard.

God then puts Jonah in a time out. He has a giant fish swallow Jonah to give him some time for self-reflection and an opportunity to change his perspective by choosing to move into the circle of choice. Jonah does just that. He recognizes that God has him where he wants him for a reason and cries out to the Lord. God recognizes that Jonah has decided to affect his life, people and circumstances and has the fish spit Jonah out onto the land.

Next, Jonah goes to Nineveh and preaches as God wanted him to. He is giving the message to the people very effectively and continues in the circle of choice. He is so effective that the people of Nineveh actually repent and change their ways. God spares them.

With the sparing of the people, Jonah again becomes the victim. He starts a passive aggressive conversation with God in an attempt to control Him. He is so used to playing the victim that he believes by pouting and telling God effectively, "See, I knew this is how you would act and I am mad so just kill me now." He thinks this victim mentality will change God's mind about sparing the people of Nineveh. It has probably worked for him in his life with other people but God sees right through it.

God teaches Jonah a final lesson by seemingly comforting Jonah with a plant for shade but then kills the plant. Jonah probably felt like he got God to grow that plant for him through playing the victim role, but God has other plans. God destroys the plant and this causes Jonah to try and use the passive aggressive victim mentality once again by asking for death as God is being unfair to him. God uses this moment to spank Jonah one last time by putting it all into scope for him. He explains what is at stake and essentially tells Jonah that he is in the victim circle and to stop doing so.

When we get hit with emotions, our typical first reaction will be to move into the Victim Circle. We see this most often in the "Pit of Despair" along the Mood Curve. We can see Jonah in the pit of despair off and on throughout the scripture verses. At this point, we have the choice to self-arrest and change how we are looking at things or stay in the Victim Circle where life, people and circumstances are happening to me. It is in the Pit of Despair that we find ourselves having to do a Moment of Truth with others and help them see their current reality. Showing someone that they are not meeting expectations can cause them to play the role of a victim. Sharing truth with grace and mercy can help prevent this but just showing them the tool can help as well.

The Two Circles can also be a good tool to help people see that they are being reactive instead of proactive. This tool can help others see that they are just reacting to the life, people and circumstances that are coming their way rather than being proactive. The proactive person is self-directed or self-governed. The person with the choice/proactive mentality will seek out new responsibility and challenges. The victim/reactive person will always need to be told what to do and will not seek out new challenges or responsibility. Showing them the Two Circles can help you share truth with them and results in a very effective MOT.

The Circle of Choice is where we choose to go to affect life, people and circumstances. It is choosing to look at things through a positive lens. It is recognizing that God has me where I am for a reason. Instead of being a victim, it is asking what I should be learning right now. Even Viktor Frankly had choices in Auschwitz and Dachau. He recognized that he could control his attitude and not play the victim. If he can do it under those circumstances, we should be able to do it when we suffer the ultimate transgression of someone cutting us off in traffic.

CHAPTER 9

Effective Communication

(HERE Tool #7)

"One should use common words to say uncommon things"—
Arthur Schopenhauer

The final tool is effective communication. This tool is the one that ties all of the others together. We have to communicate to have clarity; clarity of the THERE and clarity of our HERE. What is the big deal about clarity? Clarity provides us unity of the mind, body and spirit. Clarity creates unity of effort in our work and in our relationships with one another. Whenever clarity is not present, consequences usually are.

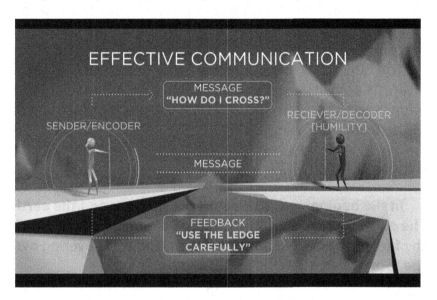

The communication model above clearly depends on the understanding of all four elements. You have to have a sender (person sending the message), a receiver (the intended audience for the message), a medium to transmit the message and feedback from the receiver.

To communicate effectively the sender must be capable of thinking clearly to be able to frame a message in a manner that will transcend the barriers to communication and the limitations of the medium. It also depends on the receiver to have humility and listen.

As we see in the Bible, God understands that clarity comes through repetition and stories. We need to hear things over and over again for them to finally sink in. Scripture does this for us. We see the same theme numerous times; God creates something perfect and good, gives it to man with clear expectations and clear consequences, man screws it up and suffers the consequences, and then God has to redeem it and make it good again. We see this with Adam and Eve in Genesis, Noah and the Ark, Moses and the Exodus, and David. This same theme continues until the unfolding of the redemptive actions of God reaches a clear climax in the coming of Jesus. With his arrival, there is a manifold increase in the witness of God. God has become man for human eyes to see and human ears to hear.

The ability to communicate and understand is God-given. The ability to miscommunicate and misunderstand is a function of our fallen condition. It is a result of focusing on ME instead of focusing on WE.

Genesis 1: 1-31

In the beginning God created the heavens and the earth. The earth was without form, and void; and darkness *was* on the face of the deep. And the Spirit of God was hovering over the face of the waters.

Then God said, "Let there be light"; and there was light. And God saw the light, that *it was* good; and God divided the light from the darkness. God called the light Day, and the darkness He called Night. So the evening and the morning were the first day.

Then God said, "Let there be a firmament in the midst of the waters, and let it divide the waters from the waters." Thus God made the firmament, and divided the waters which *were* under the firmament from the waters which *were* above the firmament; and it was so. And God called the firmament Heaven. So the evening and the morning were the second day.

Then God said, "Let the waters under the heavens be gathered together into one place, and let the dry *land* appear"; and it was so. And God called the dry *land* Earth, and the gathering together of the waters He called Seas. And God saw that *it was* good.

Then God said, "Let the earth bring forth grass, the herb *that* yields seed, *and* the fruit tree *that* yields fruit according to its kind, whose seed *is* in itself, on the earth"; and it was so. And the earth brought forth grass, the herb *that* yields seed according to its kind, and the tree *that* yields fruit, whose seed *is* in itself according to its kind. And God saw that *it was* good. So the evening and the morning were the third day.

Then God said, "Let there be lights in the firmament of the heavens to divide the day from the night; and let them be for signs and seasons, and for days and years; and let them be for lights in the firmament of the heavens to give light on the earth"; and it was so. Then God made two great lights: the greater light to rule the day, and the lesser light to rule the night. *He made* the stars also. God set them in the firmament of the heavens to give light on the earth, and to rule over the day and over the night, and to divide the light from the darkness. And God saw that *it was* good. So the evening and the morning were the fourth day.

Then God said, "Let the waters abound with an abundance of living creatures, and let birds fly above the earth across the face of the firmament of the heavens." So God created great sea creatures and every living thing that moves, with which the waters abounded, according to their kind, and every winged bird according to its kind. And God saw that *it was* good. And God blessed them, saying, "Be fruitful and multiply, and fill the waters in the seas, and let birds multiply on the earth." So the evening and the morning were the fifth day.

Then God said, "Let the earth bring forth the living creature according to its kind: cattle and creeping thing and beast of the earth, *each* according to its kind"; and it was so. And God made the beast of the earth according to its kind, cattle according to its kind, and everything that creeps on the earth according to its kind. And God saw that *it was* good.

Then God said, "Let Us make man in Our image, according to Our likeness; let them have dominion over the fish of the sea, over the birds of the air, and over the cattle, over all the earth and over every creeping thing that creeps on the earth." So God created man in His *own* image; in the image of God He created him; male and female He created them. Then God blessed them, and God said to them, "Be fruitful and multiply; fill the earth and subdue it; have dominion over the fish of the sea, over the birds of the air, and over every living thing that moves on the earth."

And God said, "See, I have given you every herb *that* yields seed which *is* on the face of all the earth, and every tree whose fruit yields seed; to you it shall be for food. Also, to every beast of the earth, to every bird of the air, and to everything that creeps on the earth, in which *there is* life, *I have given* every green herb for food"; and it was so Then God saw everything that He had made, and indeed *it was* very good. So the evening and the morning were the sixth day.

From the scripture reading above, we can clearly see that when God speaks he can create. When you speak, are you creating or do you speak to destroy? Do you communicate to build relationships and serve others or do you communicate to spread rumors and talk bad about others?

All of this shows how difficult it can be to communicate clearly. The communication model will help the understanding and help us become clearer when we use it properly. The model begins with the sender.

The Sender

The sender is the first component in the communication model. For the sender to be able to communicate clearly, he must have clarity within himself. The sender needs to find the clarity of mind, body and spirit to communicate as clearly as possible. This is simply using our systems thinking to achieve this. Think back to the story of George Washington and the Newburg Address. He took the time (5 days) to try and find enough clarity within himself. He shifted from system one into systems two and three to find the words to help defuse the situation. It was ultimately his system 3 that played the biggest role and changed history for us. Once the sender has internal clarity of what he wants to communicate, he has to consider the barriers to communication that are present, the medium in which to transmit the message and to whom he is sending the message. Having considered this, the sender encodes the message to be transmitted.

Barriers

The sender must consider which barriers to communication are present to be able to frame the message in a manner that can be understood. There are numerous barriers to communication that we can run into when trying to communicate clearly. Some barriers include age, gender, position, physical size or presence, physical distance, culture and even language.

When there is an age difference, the younger person may be a bit intimidated when trying to provide feedback and may be less likely to communicate openly. The same is true with larger or louder people. Position is always easy to see. This barrier is one of the most prevalent. We are less likely to communicate as effectively with the people we report to because we are worried about our jobs or how they may perceive us.

If the sender understands the barriers well enough, he can transmit the message in a manner that can transcend those barriers. Knowing that you are sending a message to an employee or child of yours will result in the position barrier. You, as the sender will need to carefully consider how the message needs to be worded to help them understand and even be proactive with asking for feedback, instead of waiting for them to freely give it. Once the sender has carefully considered how to send the message through the barriers to effective communication, he must now consider the medium in which to send the message.

Medium

As part of the system two and three thinking, the sender should consider the medium available to transmit the message. Some of the mediums we communicate through include written word through one way mediums like magazines, news articles, letters and even books. They also include two-way written word that can provide immediate feedback like email and text messaging. We can communicate with voice over the phone. We can also communicate in person.

When selecting a medium to communicate through, the sender should select the method that will give the message the best chance for the receiver to understand it. This method may be driven by other factors like barriers to communication. We know that face to face communication is almost always going to be the most effective. This is because we can read body language, hear tone of voice and communicate rapidly. We may not have the luxury to communicate in this manner due to physical distance or the message being time sensitive.

The dangers of transmitting a message through a medium other than face to face communication compound dramatically. Do you use email in your everyday communication? Do your emails ever get misinterpreted? Do you use text messaging in your everyday communication? How much more does that get misinterpreted? We can easily recognize that the receiver of our text or email can easily read inflection or attitude into it without it ever being the intent. This could lead to a completely different interpretation by the receiver.

Receiver

The final piece of the equation for effective communication is the receiver. The receiver has to listen and decode the message and then provide feedback. The receiver must have the humility to lay himself aside and try to understand the intended intent of the receiver's message without reading into it and changing the meaning.

Listening can be very difficult. Most of us think we are very good listeners but that just shows how far we are from our current reality (HERE). How do you know if you are a good listener? The same way you know your HERE. You have your perspective, get other perspectives and try to find the truth based on them. I just ask my wife and she tells me that I am a terrible listener. There are a lot of components that tie into listening.

One of the best ways to learn to listen effectively is to practice Observational Listening. Experts used to use the term active listening which pointed you in the direction of asking questions. We now use observational listening which can be even more effective. Observational listening occurs when the listener focuses on the sender and makes a mental movie in his head about the story that is being told. This takes a good deal of effort. You have to have humility. You have to have external focus and not focus on what you are going to say next. Making the movie in your head helps you focus on them instead of you.

As we continue listening and make the mental movie in our head, we also ask questions to clarify the mental image. The rule of thumb is that in a mentoring setting we should ask four questions to every one statement. In a teaching situation we should ask one question to every four statements. When we mentor, we want to guide the other person to self-discovery, learning through the question process. When teaching, we are just trying to keep the other person or people engaged and following along.

When we learn to listen through our System 3 or Renewed Mind, we can better understand what God wants us to do. Sometimes the Holy Spirit speaks very clearly to us when we listen well. Learning to listen to what God is telling us requires humility and focus.

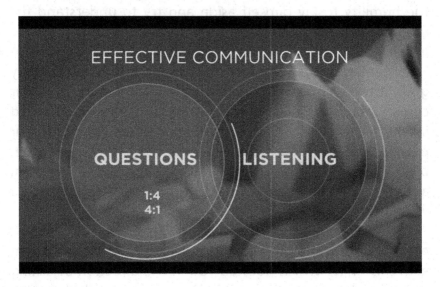

James 1: 19-27

So then, my beloved brethren, let every man be swift to hear, slow to speak, slow to wrath; for the wrath of man does not produce the righteousness of God.

Therefore lay aside all filthiness and overflow of wickedness, and receive with meekness the implanted word, which is able to save your souls.

But be doers of the word, and not hearers only, deceiving yourselves. For if anyone is a hearer of the word and not a doer, he is like a man observing his natural face in a mirror; for he observes himself, goes away, and immediately forgets what kind of man he was. But he who looks into the perfect law of liberty and continues *in it,* and is not a forgetful hearer but a doer of the work, this one will be blessed in what he does.

If anyone among you thinks he is religious, and does not bridle his tongue but deceives his own heart, this one's religion *is* useless. Pure and undefiled religion before God and the Father is this: to visit orphans and widows in their trouble, *and* to keep oneself unspotted from the world.

James tells us that there are times when listening seldom occurs. We seldom listen when we are angry, want to punish the person speaking, when we don't suspend our opinion, we aren't focused on the other person or we don't make time.

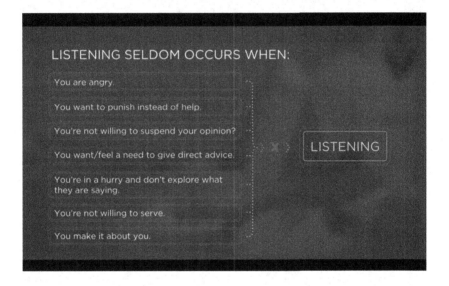

LISTENING SELDOM OCCURS WHEN:

You are angry.

You want to punish instead of help.

You're not willing to suspend your opinion?

You want/feel a need to give direct advice.

You're in a hurry and don't explore what they are saying.

You're not willing to serve.

You make it about you.

LISTENING

WHEN LISTENING, **DON'T DO** THE FOLLOWING:

LISTENING   ✗

- Try to talk the speaker into/out of feelings.
- Sympathize.
- Control the conversation.
- Give advice.
- Judge.
- Replace the speakers story with yours.

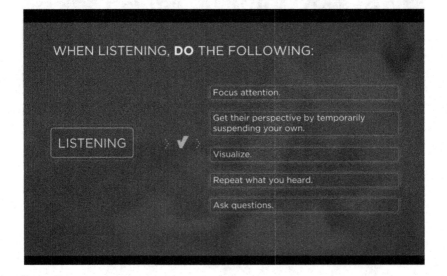

WHEN LISTENING, **DO** THE FOLLOWING:

LISTENING   ✔

- Focus attention.
- Get their perspective by temporarily suspending your own.
- Visualize.
- Repeat what you heard.
- Ask questions.

Being able to focus on the person who is communicating, make the mental image or movie of what they are saying, and ask enough questions to get the clarity you need in order to truly understand their message takes a tremendous amount of humility. It takes love. Humility is laying oneself aside and love is pursuing the best for others patiently, kindly, sacrificially and unconditionally. This is true of learning to listen to the Holy Spirit as well. When we listen through being humble and focusing on what God would have us do by praying and being in scripture, we find that the Holy Spirit finds ways to communicate with us. It may be through someone we know saying the right thing at the right time. It may come through the written Word. Or it may come through music, a sunrise, time alone, the majesty of the mountains, the expanse of the desert or any of our other surroundings.

The formula for listening is to first have the humility to not make the conversation about ME. Next, we want to focus on the other person. Make the mental movie in your head and focus on what they are saying and not on what you are going to say next. Finally, we want to be curious. We want to ask good clarifying questions that will bring that image in our minds as close to the speaker's perspective as we can. When we do those three things, we get the other person's perspective. We see what they see. This is an act of love.

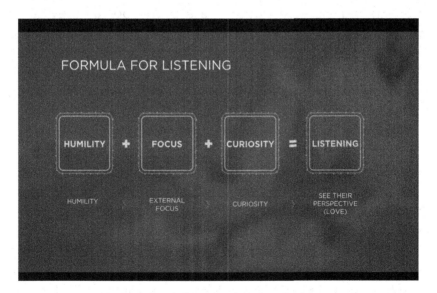

Feedback

Once the receiver listens and decodes the true meaning of the message, they now become the sender and begin to ask questions to help clarify even further. This is feedback. The receiver (now the sender) should shift into system two or three and attempt to serve the new receiver. The sender has to figure out how to transmit a message through a medium and barriers to communication so that the true meaning can be understood by the receiver...the process continues.

The best feedback can come through our actions. As James stated in the scripture reading, we should be doers of the word. When the sender sees that you are doing things differently, they know you received the message and decoded it properly. Your actions speak louder than your words.

Think back to our story of Little Round Top. Right before the charge down the hill, Chamberlain gathered his commanders together and explained to them what he wanted done. He used an analogy they all understood. He told them to have the flanking element swing like a barn door as they came down the hill so they would be on line together to press into the enemy. He used words that everyone could understand. He didn't try to say it in some strategic level military term that would make him look smart. He said it in a manner they could all understand.

Abraham Lincoln was known for his communicating ability. He said, "They say I tell a great many stories. I reckon I do; but I have learned from long experience that plain people, take them as they run, are more easily influenced through the medium of broad and humorous illustration than in any other way."

Lincoln was known as the great communicator because he understood the communication model. He listened well, taught lessons through stories and parables, used many analogies and asked a lot of questions. He left us with a great example to follow. Lincoln himself took these lessons from scripture. He was only following the example of Jesus.

Lincoln understood that when trying to communicate it is about getting the message through barriers and getting the feedback to know it was understood. He understood that effective communication is not about the sender trying to make himself look smart. It is not about how complex of a sentence structure he can create to make sure that everyone knows he's smart. Lincoln knew that communication is not about serving ME. It's about serving the person you are communicating with.

Let's look at some examples of when this is the most difficult for us. We will say the communication model is being used by two people who are very different. Two people who always struggle to communicate and never really know why. The two people we will use even communicate through the easiest medium to transmit through, face to face. However, they have the most difficult barrier to communication to overcome. They are husband and wife. Gender seems to be the most difficult of all the barriers for us to overcome.

Gender

There are significant differences to how men and women process information and communicate. Women express themselves with words where men do not. Research shows that women speak between 20,000-33,000 words per day as compared to the paltry 7,000 spoken by men. This is best explained by watching small children play. Girls spend all of their play time expressing themselves with words as they play. If you observe them play with their dolls, you quickly notice that all of the dolls have a name, they are all about to get married and have kids and a career and have really long conversations with each other that don't add up to much. Conversely, when you watch a young boy play with his cars you won't hear a single word. You hear, "Vroom" and the screech that tires make as the car accelerates but not much is expressed with words. This trait holds true as we get older.

As we age, women continue to express themselves with words and men do not. Women will talk through the entire gambit of things that happen in a day where men prefer to not express themselves through words. When asked about her day, she will spend the next ten to fifteen minutes describing it in, what some men might consider, painstaking detail. Conversely, when asked about his day, he will say, "It was fine." And that's it. This can cause some problems with our relationships. She may feel he doesn't want to open up to her and he may feel that when she is saying all this stuff, she must need him to fix something.

Men tend to feel that if there is something important enough to be said then it must require an action of some sort and they are needed to fix something for her. Of course, that is rarely the case. She is just expressing herself and ultimately just wants him to listen. Let take a look at an old Dave Berry Article.

SHE DRIVES FOR A RELATIONSHIP. HE'S LOST IN THE TRANSMISSION

—By DAVE BARRY

Let's say a guy named Roger is attracted to a woman named Elaine. He asks her out to a movie; she accepts; they have a pretty good time. A few nights later he asks her out to dinner, and again they enjoy themselves. They continue to see each other regularly, and after a while neither one of them is seeing anybody else.

And then, one evening when they're driving home, a thought occurs to Elaine, and, without really thinking, she says it aloud: "Do you realize that, as of tonight, we've been seeing each other for exactly six months?"

And then there is silence in the car. To Elaine, it seems like a very loud silence. She thinks to herself: Geez, I wonder if it bothers him that I said that. Maybe he's been feeling confined by our relationship; maybe he thinks I'm trying to push him into some kind of obligation that he doesn't want, or isn't sure of.

And Roger is thinking: Gosh. Six months.

And Elaine is thinking: But, hey, I'm not so sure I want this kind of relationship, either. Sometimes I wish I had a little more space, so I'd have time to think about whether I really want us to keep going the way we are, moving steadily toward... I mean, where are we going? Are we just going to keep seeing each other at this level of intimacy? Are we heading toward marriage? Toward children? Toward a lifetime together? Am I ready for that level of commitment? Do I really even know this person?

And Roger is thinking:... so that means it was... let's see... February when we started going out, which was right after I had the car at the dealer's, which means... lemme check the odometer... Whoa! I am way over due for an oil change here.

And Elaine is thinking: He's upset. I can see it on his face. Maybe I'm reading this completely wrong. Maybe he wants more from our relationship, more intimacy, more commitment; maybe he has sensed—even before I sensed it—that I was feeling some reservations. Yes, I bet that's it. That's why he's so reluctant to say anything about his own feelings. He's afraid of being rejected.

And Roger is thinking: And I'm gonna have them look at the transmission again. I don't care what those morons say, it's still not shifting right. And they better not try to blame it on the cold weather this time. What cold weather? It's 87 degrees out, and this thing is shifting like a garbage truck, and I paid those incompetent thieves $600.

David Kuhnert

COMMUNICATIONS GAP

And Elaine is thinking: He's angry. And I don't blame him. I'd be angry, too. God, I feel so guilty, putting him through this, but I can't help the way I feel. I'm just not sure.

And Roger is thinking: They'll probably say it's only a 90-day warranty. That's exactly what they're gonna say, the scumballs.

And Elaine is thinking: Maybe I'm just too idealistic, waiting for a knight to come riding up on his white horse, when I'm sitting right next to a perfectly good person, a person I enjoy being with, a person I truly do care about, a person who seems to truly care about me. A person who is in pain because of my school girl romantic fantasy.

And Roger is thinking: Warranty? They want a warranty? I'll give them a warranty. I'll take their warranty and stick it right up their...

"Roger," Elaine says aloud.

"What?" says Roger, startled.

"Please don't torture yourself like this," she says, her eyes beginning to brim with tears. "Maybe I should never have... Oh God, I feel so..." (She breaks down, sobbing.)

"What?" says Roger.

"I'm such a fool," Elaine sobs. "I mean, I know there's no knight. I really know that. It's silly. There's no knight, and there's no horse."

"There's no horse?" says Roger.

"You think I'm a fool, don't you?" Elaine says.

"No!" says Roger, glad to finally know the correct answer.

"It's just that... It's that I... I need some time," Elaine says. (There is a 15-second pause while Roger, thinking as fast as he can, tries to come up with a safe response. Finally he comes up with one that he thinks might work.)

"Yes," he says.

A BEFUDDLED BEAU

(Elaine, deeply moved, touches his hand.)

"Oh, Roger, do you really feel that way?" she says.

"What way?" says Roger.

"That way about time," says Elaine.

"Oh," says Roger. "Yes." (Elaine turns to face him and gazes deeply into his eyes, causing him to become very nervous about what she might say next, especially if it involves a horse. At last she speaks.)

"Thank you, Roger," she says.

"Thank you," says Roger. Then he takes her home, and she lies on her bed, a conflicted, tortured soul, and weeps until dawn, whereas when Roger gets back to his place, he opens a bag of Doritos, turns on the TV, and immediately becomes deeply involved in a rerun of a tennis match between two Czechoslovakians he never heard of. A tiny voice in the far recesses of his mind tells him that something major was going on back there in the car, but he is pretty sure there is no way he would ever understand what, and so he figures it's better if he doesn't think about it. (This is also Roger's policy regarding world hunger.)

IT'S ANALYSIS TIME

The next day Elaine will call her closest friend, or perhaps two of them, and they will talk about this situation for six straight hours. In painstaking detail, they will analyze everything she said and everything he said, going over it time and time again, exploring every word, expression, and gesture for nuances of meaning, considering every possible ramification. They will continue to discuss this subject, off and on, for weeks, maybe months, never reaching any definite conclusions, but never getting bored with it, either.

Meanwhile, Roger, while playing racquetball one day with a mutual friend of his and Elaine's, will pause just before serving, frown, and say: "Norm, did Elaine ever own a horse?"

Although the article is funny, it is also true. We have to understand how each person processes information to be able to understand what is happening. Men should remember that just because she is talking incessantly about something does not necessarily mean it is an action item. Just listen. Women have to realize that men typically want to be that "knight in shining armor" for her. So, when he tries to fix things, he is trying to serve her.

Clarity

We have to communicate in almost everything we do. When we find that our systems thinking is working we will have internal clarity of mind, body and spirit. From there, we can start to focus on the receiver of our message and communicate the message in a manner in which will produce the desired response. This means that sometimes we have to say things differently than we would like to in order to avoid the receiver misinterpreting the message. We sometimes like to make ourselves sound smart so we say things in a manner that we think will accomplish this. This does not serve the other person. It only serves ME.

In order to have clarity of your THERE, you must communicate it with your team. If your spouse doesn't know your THERE, it is hard for them to support you in it. Clarity comes through communication. When we communicate poorly or don't listen, we will not have clarity. When clarity is absent, you will always find a degree of consequence.

The ability to communicate and be understood is God-given. Miscommunicating and not being understood is a result of our fallen condition. Repetition in communication is necessary as it takes seven to eleven times to hear something before we finally get it.

The communication model is made up of the sender, receiver, medium and barriers to communication. The sender must have internal clarity before he is able to communicate with external clarity. He must consider the medium through which to transmit the message and the barriers to communication that are present.

The receiver has to listen. Listening takes humility and results in love. We should use observational listening when others are talking. Once the receiver thinks he understands the message, he provides feedback by becoming the sender.

CHAPTER 10

The Structure and Seven Tools in One

(TYING IT ALL TOGETHER)

As you have probably already gleaned, these seven tools and one structure, although taught separately, are in reality intertwined. They work together and are more difficult to teach separately than as one large tool. However, the human minds needs smaller chunks with stories and repetition to help us remember and understand.

The picture below represents how it would all look on one slide. It can look overwhelming so let's talk through it.

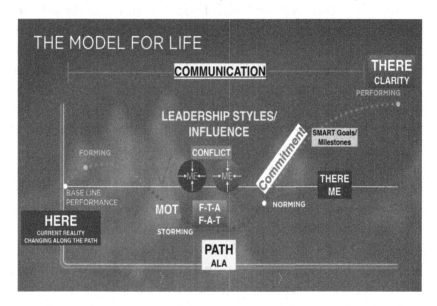

The structure for life is THERE-HERE-PATH. We have to have clarity of the THERE, current reality of the HERE and commitment for the PATH where we will have to Act/Learn/Adjust along the way. Our definition of leadership is influencing others to get THERE.

Clarity of the THERE is potentially the most important item. Clarity comes from internal harmony and unity of the systems thinking and the five whys. Once we can establish our transcendent THERE, we have to communicate it with others. We use the communication model of sender, receiver, medium and barriers to communication to be able to help others with clarity. The sender uses systems thinking to become internally clear and then considers the receiver to send the message in a manner that will not be misinterpreted. The sender chooses the best medium available and considers the barriers that are present and how best to work around them. The receiver must listen with observational listening. This requires humility and the will to serve others. He will then become the sender through asking clarifying questions.

Once we know the THERE we have to know our current reality, our HERE. We have five forms of influence which are position, coercive, reward, expert and referent. Referent power is the most influential of the five. The tenets of referent power are physical, social, mental/emotional, family/team, spiritual and financial. The foundation for the tenets of referent power is your values. We deliver our influence through the five leadership styles. We have directive, transactional, participative, delegative and transformational.

The PATH is the project mood curve. It connects our HERE to our THERE. Every step we take along the PATH our HERE changes. It has to constantly be reevaluated. Along the path we find the pit of despair. No matter what we undertake, we will always find the pit of despair. The only difference between your pit and the next person's pit will be the depth. Understanding that the pit will be there can help us recognize it as a part of learning and progression. These are the difficult moments where conflict, moment of truth and the two circles usually come into play. We also find that this is where we experience the most intense emotions. We deal with the emotions with feel-act think or feel-think-act. However, if we are in the circle of choice we will look at the pit of despair as an opportunity to lead. The pit is where leadership happens. This is also where we tend to find that we need more structure or less structure so we use the Freedom "V" and evaluate whether we are trying to control ourselves or control others.

We need milestones along the PATH to keep us moving toward the THERE. These milestones should be SMART. They can be our pillars or our values but we want them to be tangible. Those milestones or SMART goals will help us form habits. Once we have made habits, those habits require less willpower or energy.

The tools are meant to serve you and serve others. Helping others find a THERE for their lives can in and of itself be transformational. However, taking it a step further and helping them clarify their HERE by utilizing one of or a combination of the seven tools could be the catalyst for change that they need in their lives. That change can help them find God or draw closer to God. When nearer to God and living life the way he intended them to, they will be able to set an example of this for others. They will in turn change the lives of others and transform not only their own lives but the lives of those around them.

I have taught this material for several years now. I inevitably will have a person who is further down the road of life than most of the others in attendance. This material will often cause them to recognize that they have not been focused on a legacy of serving others and transforming others. They will often say, "I wish I would have known this material 50 years ago." My message to those of you who find yourself in this boat is simple. It comes from Jesus himself.

Matthew 20: 1-16

"For the kingdom of heaven is like a landowner who went out early in the morning to hire laborers for his vineyard. Now when he had agreed with the laborers for a denarius a day, he sent them into his vineyard. And he went out about the third hour and saw others standing idle in the marketplace, and said to them, 'You also go into the vineyard, and whatever is right I will give you.' So they went. Again he went out about the sixth and the ninth hour, and did likewise. And about the eleventh hour he went out and found others standing idle, and said to them, 'Why have you been standing here idle all

day?' They said to him, 'Because no one hired us.' He said to them, 'You also go into the vineyard, and whatever is right you will receive.'

"So when evening had come, the owner of the vineyard said to his steward, 'Call the laborers and give them *their* wages, beginning with the last to the first.' And when those came who *were hired* about the eleventh hour, they each received a denarius. But when the first came, they supposed that they would receive more; and they likewise received each a denarius. And when they had received *it*, they complained against the landowner, saying, 'These last *men* have worked *only* one hour, and you made them equal to us who have borne the burden and the heat of the day.' But he answered one of them and said, 'Friend, I am doing you no wrong. Did you not agree with me for a denarius? Take *what is* yours and go your way. I wish to give to this last man *the same* as to you. Is it not lawful for me to do what I wish with my own things? Or is your eye evil because I am good?' So the last will be first, and the first last. For many are called, but few chosen."

Take heart in the fact that although you may have been called late you are still called and your reward will be the same as those who were called early. Use the spiritual gifts you have been given and serve others. Serve them through your example for your remaining days. Serve them through demonstrating what it means to do life right. Show others what it means to be a Servant Leader who leads a transformational life.

Practical Application

Over the years I have had the opportunity to serve some amazing men in and out of the Army. I often get asked what the difference is in leadership between the military and civilian world. The answer is very simple. Our military leaders get their 10,000 hours of application much sooner than most professions in the civilian community. Our first responders in the civilian community would be a close second. It isn't just the frequency that you are applying this leadership by example but also the intensity. In the military, lives are on the line all the time. The intensity that this brings causes that application to be intensely focused.

Most of the soldiers I know who got out of the Army or retired as I have, would trade almost anything to go back in and serve. Many of them suffer from post-traumatic stress disorder or some kind of a depression but they would gladly rejoin their units and deploy today. They have suffered a tremendous amount physically, mentally or both and would gladly go back into the Army and serve. What would drive a man to do this? That is the question that most of them struggle to answer as well.

Maslow's Hierarchy of Needs can help us understand the answer to that question a little better. The basest need we have is physiological. This is food, water and sleep. Once those needs are met, we look for safety. We accomplish this through shelter from the elements or other dangers. The third need in the pyramid starts to enter the realm of higher needs. The need for belonging and love. This is why most men would go back in the Army and put it all on the line again. This is why many suffer from depression. They were a part of something that cannot be replicated under normal conditions in the civilian community. Most were a part of a 30-40 man platoon that lived, ate, fought and died together. They were part of a family whose members were ready to die for one another without thought. They loved and served one another on a daily basis.

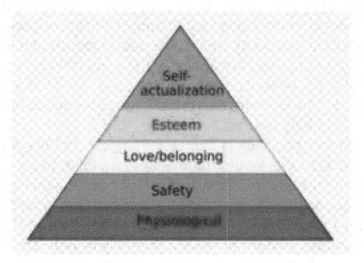

After leaving the military, men who were tired of deployments and the fast-paced life miss the family they had there. Serving/loving others is a part of what is expected of you every day in the military. It is the culture of the platoon to stand by one another at all times. It's easy to serve others in this type of environment. Serving each other is just what you do and if you don't do it people get hurt or die. The opportunities to serve others happens all of the time. The level of fulfillment we get from serving others or loving others as part of this is very addicting. We feel good about serving others to the point where we want to keep doing it. This is the reward that God has planted in that act selflessness for us but when they rejoin the civilian work force, it is harder to do.

When these men rejoin the civilian community, they cannot and do not find the same level of comradery or brotherhood they had in the military. They are searching for others to serve in the same capacity and with the same level of intensity of which they had in the military. However, that level is much harder to find. What was easy to find in the military is not as prevalent in the civilian community. It is there but it is harder to find and it will not be with the same level of intensity. The structure that they had in the military to serve others isn't present anymore and if they don't create their own, new structure, that unfulfilled depression will continue.

Some of the issue is also the addiction to the adrenaline one feels when in harm's way. However, just understanding what you are going through can make it easier to cope with. It is similar to the Mood Curve. Just knowing you are in it (you're here) can help prevent it from becoming as deep. Understanding that you are looking for the fulfillment that comes from serving others coupled with some adrenaline can help you create a structure that fulfills both of these things.

My recommendation for those going through reintegration issues from the military or from time abroad on mission trips or just being away for a long period is the same. Get involved with a group or organization that is about serving others. For veterans, it may be the VFW, American Legion or Disabled Veterans. For others, it may be church planting, Big Brother/ Big Sister or any other organizations that provides a structure to serve people.

Doing these service oriented tasks do a couple of things for you. First, it takes the focus off of ME and puts it on WE. This is what God asked us to do and if you do them, you will once again be moving towards your THERE. Focusing on your THERE will take the oscillating effect out of your PATH and help you find internal contentment and joy. Second, you will get the benefit of a strong social pillar of servant minded people who are going through similar struggles. Most veterans tend to believe that no one else will understand what they are going through. Usually they feel that way because they don't know what they are going through either. Finding others who are struggling and talking about it can help them figure out why they are struggling and what the next step down the PATH should look like.

Choosing to stay in the pit of despair and being a victim will result in no progress down the PATH. It will result in a ME-centric life that will continue to only focus on ME. These people are not fun to be around as they tend to ruin the relationships with those they encounter. Instead, focus on WE and serving others. This allows us the freedom to maneuver down the PATH towards the THERE.

I have spent a great deal of time dealing with guys who suffer from PTSD or survivor's remorse. This too can be helped in a similar manner as the depression. I remember the only time that I ever cried in combat. It was when we were having guys get hurt frequently and there was nothing I could do about it. I wanted control. I was frustrated. It took me months to realize that God is the only one in control. He is the only one that can stop bad things from happening. Once I let go of trying to control things, it changed my attitude and then of course my actions. I was free from ME. I was able to be a better example of resiliency. I was able to better lead by example.

People who suffer from survivor's remorse are going through this same thing. Trusting that God is in charge is the only way out of this pit of despair. Believing that God has preserved your life for some reason and that you better make it worth it, is the best mindset to have. I should have been killed scores of times over. Whether it was due to a new piece of equipment, poor timing from the enemy or just taking a left instead of a right, I somehow survived. This statistical improbability would say that I am very lucky or God has a plan for me. I spent a long time asking the same questions as survivor's remorse sufferers. Why wasn't I with them when it happened? How come I survived the blast and they didn't? I would do anything to change places with them. All of these are logical questions and statements but we have to go back to the first thing we can control. Do I trust God or someone other than God?

If I trust God and believe He is in control, then He has His plan for me. To not try to live the best life I can and find meaning in my life of serving would be to dishonor God and those I left behind. I owe it to them to live the best life I possibly can and find a way to make it count by influencing others to get THERE.

Using this simple THP structure and the seven tools can help get your life back on track or help someone else do the same. Being an example of how to live life the way God intended us to, is the best way to execute the Great Commission. Living a Servant Leader life will attract others to you. They will see your resiliency and fulfillment in life and want to be like you. You can now share these tools with them and arm them with this basic understanding to serve and mentor others.

My hope and prayer is for this simple understanding of life tools to serve you in some manner and that you will be better equipped to serve others. The idea is for you to be able to take these tools and have a more fulfilled life. This is meant to be the catalyst for change in your life and not a simple book to read. The next time you hit the pit of despair, may you stay committed to your THERE and lead through your personal example like Joshua Chamberlain. May you communicate like Lincoln and be able to serve others like Washington. Ultimately, may you find yourself more Christ-like.-God Bless!

ACKNOWLEDGEMENTS

"That which has been is what will be, that which is done is what will be done, and there is nothing new under the sun."- Ecclesiastes 1: 9 NKJV.

As the writer of Ecclesiastes so eloquently wrote, there is nothing new under the sun. None of this material is new either. However, there are several books and people who have spent many hours packaging these concepts. We only took those concepts and tried to put them into a more memorable and usable format.

HTP for this book

Much of this material was adopted from Hermann Eben's GR8 Leaders and GR8 Relationship courses. Hermann is a Leadership Consultant who owns and operates Trimtab Solutions. Hermann teaches these courses all over the world. I would highly recommend these courses to every business or social organization. Without Hermann and his life-long work, this book would not be possible.

From Hermann's material, a group of really great people, led by Tim Dunn, started getting together on their Saturdays to put together a trimmed down version that might be easier to digest and be more cross-cultural. From Tim's group of Brandon and Laura Shuman, Tim and Valerie Bowden, Chris Hsiao, Jonny and Sarah Custer and myself came the beginning versions of this product. Without these amazing people, this book would not have been possible. The HERE was that we felt like we needed Hermann's material to be easier to digest. So our THERE was to create a program that could cross gender, cultural and age boundaries. From this came the business version of a Servant Leadership Class.

After putting together a business version of this material, two good people took this material to the field on a mission trip. Joey and Kylie Grabauskas spent 11 months teaching the material to dozens of other missionaries as part of the World Race. They proved the material in different cultures, ages and genders. They showed me how transformational these tools can really be. I could not be more proud of them and the impact that they have had on changing the lives of so many people.

God continued to speak to me through Tim Dunn and his Sunday school classes at Midland Bible Church. Whether it would be a part of Tim's teaching or something the pastor, Mark Rae, said in a sermon, God kept showing me these tools throughout scripture and life. I was being nudged by the Holy Spirit to start putting together a non-secular version of the same Servant Leadership Class.

Soon thereafter, a good friend of mine, Chris Seegers, motivated me to start that non-secular version. Once I completed the classroom version, my family became the first guinea pigs. Without my wife Beth, and my children Joseph Kuhnert, Katherine Summer, Amanda Kuhnert, Elizabeth and Casey Galerneau and Aaron Rossman and all of their encouragement and support, I may not have ever undertaken this book.

It's easy to see from the previous four paragraphs that God has been at work here. To Him goes all of the glory. He is the one at work and He placed all of these amazing people in my life to influence me to get THERE.

SOURCES

Hermann Eben-Leadership Consultant for Trimtab Solutions, Teacher for *GR8 Leaders and GR8 Relationships Course*, Friend and Mentor.

The U.S. Army Leadership Field Manual: FM 22-100. Indianapolis, Ind.?: BN, 2008.

Bodaken, Bruce, and Robert Fritz. *The Managerial Moment of Truth*: The Essential Step in Helping People Improve Performance. New York: Free, 2006. Print.

Covey, Stephen R. *The 7 Habits of Highly Effective People: Powerful Lessons in Personal Change.* N.p.: n.p., n.d. Print.

Baumeister, Roy F., and John Tierney. *Willpower: Rediscovering the Greatest Human Strength.* New York: Penguin, 2011. Print.

Phillips, Donald T. *Lincoln on Leadership: Executive Strategies for Tough times.* New York: Warner, 1992. Print.

Fritz, Robert. *The Path of Least Resistance: Learning to Become the Creative Force in Your Own Life.* New York: Ballantine, 1989. Print.

Kahneman, Daniel. *Thinking, Fast and Slow.* N.p.: n.p., n.d. Print.

Collins, James C. *Good to Great: Why Some Companies Make the Leap... and Others Don't.* New York, NY: HarperBusiness, 2001. Print.

Catmull, Edwin E., and Amy Wallace. *Creativity, Inc.: Overcoming the Unseen Forces That Stand in the Way of True Inspiration*. N.p.: n.p., n.d. Print.

Senge, Peter M. *The Fifth Discipline Fieldbook*. London: N. Brealey, 1994. Print.

Frankl, Viktor E. *Man's Search for Meaning*. N.p.: n.p., n.d. Print.

Carnegie, Dale. *How to Win Friends and Influence People*. New York: Simon and Schuster, 1981. Print.

God, **the Holy Bible**. Beginning of time.